Mini Crochet Creatures

30 AMIGURUMI ANIMALS TO MAKE

LAUREN BERGSTROM

First published 2018 by
Guild of Master Craftsman Publications Ltd
Castle Place, 166 High Street, Lewes,
East Sussex BN7 1XU

ISBN 978 1 78494 389 9

A catalogue record for this book is available
from the British Library.

Publisher Jonathan Bailey
Production Manager Jim Bulley
Senior Project Editor Dominique Page
Editor Nicola Hodgson
Managing Art Editor Gilda Pacitti
Designer Luana Gobbo
Photographer & Illustrator Lauren Bergstrom

Colour origination by GMC Reprographics
Printed and bound in China

Contents

Introduction 8

Farm animals 10
Chick 12
Chicken 16
Cow 20
Piglet 24
Sheep 28

Pet animals 32
Bunny 34
Cat 38
Dog 42
Goldfish 46
Guinea pig 50

Sea animals 54
Penguin 56
Otter 60
Sea bunny 64
Seal 68
Whale 72

Little animals 76
Butterfly 78
Caterpillar 82
Honey bee 86
Ladybird 90
Snail 94

Woodland animals 98
Bear 100
Fox 104
Owl 108
Raccoon 112
Squirrel 116

Zoo animals 120
Elephant 122
Hippo 126
Lion 130
Panda 134
Sloth 138

Tools and materials 142
Techniques 144
Abbreviations and
  conversions 154
Suppliers and
  resources 156
About the author 157
Index 158

Introduction

Make your very own miniature menagerie with these 30 amigurumi animal patterns.

All of the animals are made with a simple, roundish body shape, with crocheted details and embroidered features. This construction makes it very easy to customize your little creature. You can experiment with different colours, sew the details on differently, or even mix and match patterns to create new animals.

These amigurumi can be made with many different types of yarn. Try using chunky yarn for a jumbo size, or lightweight yarn for a really tiny version. If you are looking for a challenge, experiment with faux fur or chenille to make extra-fluffy animals. Since each project uses only a small amount of yarn, this is a good way to try new things, or use up bits of yarn left over from other projects.

Amigurumi animals can be of practical use, too. You can use them as pin cushions, turn them into keychains or hanging ornaments, string them together on a garland, or make them into a hanging mobile. They look adorable displayed on a shelf or in a shadow box, and would make lovely gifts.

Each little creature takes about one or two hours to crochet, so making one is a quick and satisfying project. You will soon find yourself with a whole horde of new amigurumi friends.

Lauren Bergstrom

Farm Animals

Actual size

Size
Using the suggested yarn and hook, your chick's body will be about 1⅜in (3.5cm) tall.

You will need
Medium-weight yarn in main colour – approx 11yd (10m)
Crochet hook – 3.5mm (UK9:USE/4)
Toy stuffing
Yarn needle
Embroidery needle
Embroidery thread
   in black and orange

Abbreviations
See page 154

Chick

These quick and easy chicks have a small body, crocheted wings and a tail. Their little faces are sewn on with embroidery thread. Baby chickens are great for using up leftover bits of yarn; you can never have too many on a farm. They have a way of multiplying when you're not paying attention.

BODY

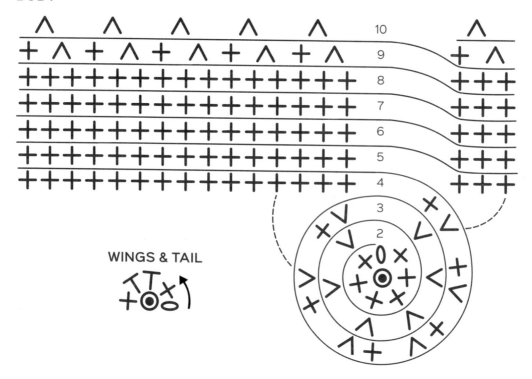

WINGS & TAIL

KEY

- ● start
- O adjustable ring
- ⬬ chain
- ⬭ slip stitch
- + double crochet
- T half treble crochet
- Ŧ treble crochet
- V 2 double crochet in 1 stitch
- ∧ double crochet 2 together

Body

The chick's body is crocheted from top to bottom. Work in the round, without joining rounds. Start with an adjustable ring.

1 6 dc into ring.

2 2 dc in each st around (12 dc).

3 (2 dc in next st, dc in next st) 6 times (18 dc).

4–8 Dc in each st around, for 5 rounds (18 dc per round).

9 (Dc2tog, dc in next st) 6 times (12 sts).
Stuff the body, making it nice and puffy.

10 (Dc2tog) 6 times (6 sts).
Cut yarn, leaving a long tail for sewing, and finish off. Add a little more stuffing if necessary, then sew the hole closed.

Wings and tail

(make 3)
Start with an adjustable ring.

1 (Dc, 2 htr, dc) into ring (4 sts).
Do not join round. Cut yarn, leaving a tail for sewing, and finish off.

Finishing

Sew the wings onto the sides of your baby chick. They should be between rounds 5 and 6 of the body, about 6 stitches apart. Sew the tail onto the back of your chick, between rounds 8 and 9 of the body. Using orange thread, sew a few straight stitches to make a small beak in the middle of the face, in line with round 5 of the body. Use black thread to sew some eyes onto the face, between rounds 4 and 5 of the body and about 3 stitches apart.

Actual size

Size

Using the suggested yarn and hook, your chicken's body will be about 2in (5cm) tall.

You will need

Medium-weight yarn in main colour
  – approx 16½yd (15m)
Medium-weight yarn in red – approx 1yd (1m)
Crochet hook – 3.5mm (UK9:USE/4)
Toy stuffing
Yarn needle
Craft felt in red
Embroidery needle
Embroidery thread in black, red and orange

Abbreviations

See page 154

Chicken

Expand your chicken coop with some fully
grown chickens. They have a blobby body, with
crocheted wings and an embroidered felt face.
A crocheted comb is sewn on top of the head
for good measure. Chickens can be made in a
variety of colours, and love to roam in flocks.

BODY

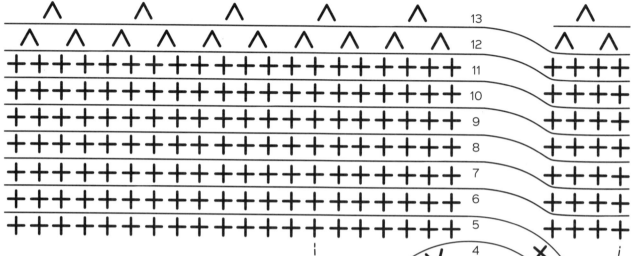

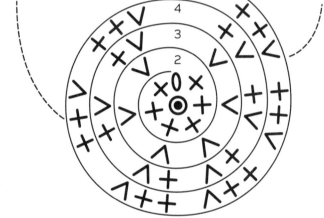

KEY

- **●** start
- **O** adjustable ring
- **⊖** chain
- **⬮** slip stitch
- **+** double crochet
- **T** half treble crochet
- **Ŧ** treble crochet
- **V** 2 double crochet in 1 stitch
- **Λ** double crochet 2 together

WINGS

TAIL

COMB

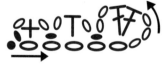

FACE TEMPLATE 100% SCALE

Body

The chicken's body is crocheted from top to bottom. Work in the round, without joining rounds. Using main colour, start with an adjustable ring.
1 6 dc into ring.
2 2 dc in each st around (12 dc).
3 (2 dc in next st, dc in next st) 6 times (18 dc).
4 (2 dc in next st, dc in next 2 sts) 6 times (24 dc).
5–11 Dc in each st around, for 7 rounds (24 dc per round).
12 (Dc2tog) 12 times (12 sts). Stuff the body, making it nice and puffy.
13 (Dc2tog) 6 times (6 sts). Cut yarn, leaving a long tail for sewing, and finish off. Add a little more stuffing if necessary, then sew the hole closed.

Wings

(make 2)
Using main colour, start with an adjustable ring.
1 (Dc, htr, 2 tr, htr, dc) into ring (6 sts).
Do not join round. Cut yarn, leaving a tail for sewing, and finish off.

Tail

Using main colour, start with an adjustable ring.
1 (Dc, 2 htr, dc) into ring (4 sts).
Do not join round. Cut yarn, leaving a tail for sewing, and finish off.

Comb

Using red yarn, ch 8.
1 (2 tr, ch 2) in 4th ch from hook, (sl st, ch 1) in next ch, (htr, ch 1) in next ch, (sl st, ch 1) in next ch, (dc, ch 1, sl st) in final ch.
Cut yarn, leaving a long tail for sewing, and finish off. If your comb seems too floppy, try using a smaller size crochet hook.

Finishing

Use the template to cut a face shape out of red craft felt. With red thread, sew the face onto the front of your chicken, in line with rounds 4 to 7 of the body. Sew the wings onto the sides of your chicken. They should be between rounds 6 and 7 of the body, about 7 stitches apart.
Sew the tail onto the back of your chicken, between rounds 10 and 11 of the body. Sew the comb on top of the head, right in the middle. The taller part of the comb should be in front.
Use black thread to embroider little eyes onto your chicken's face. Use orange thread to sew a tiny beak.

Actual size

Size

Using the suggested yarn and hook, your cow's body will be about 2in (5cm) long.

You will need

Medium-weight yarn in main colour – approx 16½yd (15m)
Medium-weight yarn in contrast colour – approx 5½yd (5m)
Medium-weight yarn in pink – approx 2yd (2m)
Medium-weight yarn in black – approx 1yd (1m)
Crochet hook – 3.5mm (UK9:USE/4)
Yarn needle
Toy stuffing
Craft felt for spots (optional)
Embroidery thread to match craft felt (optional)
Embroidery needle (optional)

Abbreviations

See page 154

Cow

Every farm needs at least one cute dairy cow.
Start with a round body, then add the crocheted
hooves, a muzzle, and some ears. Cows can come in
solid colours or with felt spots to differentiate
them - you decide how you want yours to look.
No two cows are ever alike.

BODY

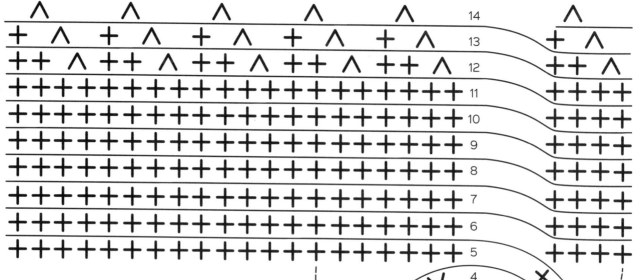

KEY

- **•** start
- **O** adjustable ring
- **⌒** chain
- **⬮** slip stitch
- **+** double crochet
- **T** half treble crochet
- **Ŧ** treble crochet
- **V** 2 double crochet in 1 stitch
- **Λ** double crochet 2 together

HOOVES

EARS

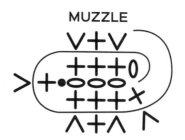

MUZZLE

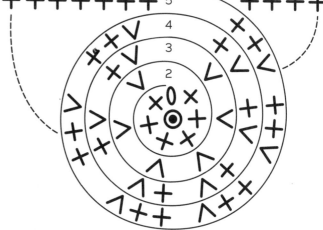

Body

The cow's body is crocheted from back to front. Work in the round, without joining rounds. Using main colour, start with an adjustable ring.

1 6 dc into ring.

2 2 dc in each st around (12 dc).

3 (2 dc in next st, dc in next st) 6 times (18 dc).

4 (2 dc in next st, dc in next 2 sts) 6 times (24 dc).

5–11 Dc in each st around, for 7 rounds (24 dc per round).

12 (Dc2tog, dc in next 2 sts) 6 times (18 sts).

13 (Dc2tog, dc in next st) 6 times (12 sts).

Stuff the body, making it nice and puffy.

14 (Dc2tog) 6 times (6 sts).

Cut yarn, leaving a long tail for sewing, and finish off. Add a little more stuffing if necessary, then sew the hole closed.

Hooves

(make 4)

Using contrast colour, start with an adjustable ring.

1 6 dc into ring.

Cut yarn, leaving a long tail for sewing, and finish off. Join round.

Muzzle

Using pink yarn, ch 4.

1 Dc in 2nd ch from hook, dc in next ch, 3 dc in last ch. Rotate your work so that you can crochet back down the bottom of the starting chain. Dc in next ch, 2 dc in last ch (8 dc).

2 2 dc in first stitch of round 1, dc in next st, 2 dc in each of next 3 sts, dc in next st, 2 dc in each of next 2 sts (14 dc).

Cut yarn, leaving a long tail for sewing, and finish off. Join round.

Ears

(make 2)

Using contrast colour, ch 3.

1 Dc in the very first ch.

Cut yarn, leaving a long tail for sewing, and finish off.

Finishing

Sew the four hooves onto the bottom of your cow. The back hooves should line up with rounds 5 and 6 of the body; the front hooves should line up with rounds 9 and 10. You can pin the hooves in place to make sure they are straight before sewing.

Sew the muzzle onto the front of your cow.

Sew the ears in place, in line with round 11 of the body and about 8 stitches apart.

Use black yarn to sew the eyes on either side of the muzzle.

Use pink yarn to sew two little horns in between the ears.

If you are adding spots, cut a few small blob shapes out of craft felt. Use a matching thread to sew the felt markings onto your cow's body.

Size

Using the suggested yarn and hook, your piglet's body will be about 2in (5cm) long.

Actual size

You will need

Medium-weight yarn in light pink – approx 22yd (20m)
Medium-weight yarn in black – approx 1yd (1m)
Crochet hook – 3.5mm (UK9:USE/4)
Toy stuffing
Yarn needle
Craft felt in pink
Embroidery needle
Embroidery thread in pink
Small two-hole button (optional)

Abbreviations

See page 154

Piglet

These little pigs are plump and round.
Their bodies are made first, then crocheted
trotters and ears are sewn in place.
Complete your amigurumi with a felt snout,
or try a small two-hole button for a cute
variation. Piglets are often found stacked
in a pile, trying to grab out-of-reach snacks.

BODY

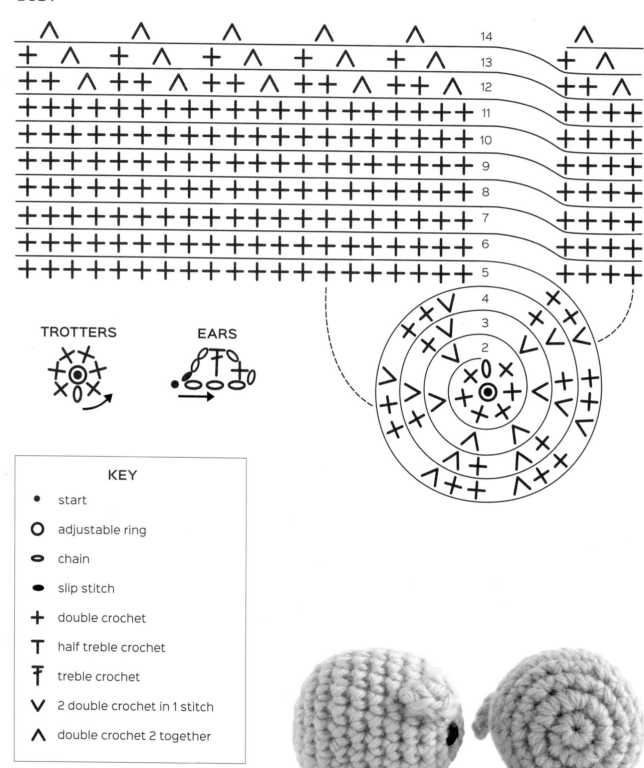

KEY

- **•** start
- **O** adjustable ring
- **⊖** chain
- **⬤** slip stitch
- **+** double crochet
- **T** half treble crochet
- **Ŧ** treble crochet
- **V** 2 double crochet in 1 stitch
- **∧** double crochet 2 together

TROTTERS

EARS

Body

The piglet's body is crocheted from back to front. Work in the round, without joining rounds. Using pink yarn, start with an adjustable ring.

1 6 dc into ring.

2 2 dc in each st around (12 dc).

3 (2 dc in next st, dc in next st) 6 times (18 dc).

4 (2 dc in next st, dc in next 2 sts) 6 times (24 dc).

5–11 Dc in each st around, for 7 rounds (24 dc per round).

12 (Dc2tog, dc in next 2 sts) 6 times (18 sts).

13 (Dc2tog, dc in next st) 6 times (12 sts).

Stuff the body, making it nice and puffy.

14 (Dc2tog) 6 times (6 sts).

Cut yarn, leaving a long tail for sewing, and finish off. Add a little more stuffing if necessary, then sew the hole closed.

Trotters

(make 4)

Using pink yarn, start with an adjustable ring.

1 6 dc into ring.

Cut yarn, leaving a long tail for sewing, and finish off. Join round.

Ears

(make 2)

Using pink yarn, ch 4.

1 (Dc, ch 1) in 2nd ch from hook, (tr, ch 2) in next ch, sl st in last ch.

Cut yarn, leaving a long tail for sewing, and finish off.

Finishing

Sew the four trotters onto the bottom of your piglet. The back trotters should line up with rounds 5 and 6 of the body; the front trotters should line up with rounds 9 and 10. You can pin them in place to make sure they are straight before sewing.

Sew the ears in place, in line with rounds 10 and 11 of the body and about 6 stitches apart.

To make a felt snout, cut a ³⁄₈in (1cm) square out of craft felt. Cut away the corners of the square to make a round shape. Use a matching thread to sew the snout onto your piglet's face, right in the middle.

Sew two small stitches for nostrils.

Alternatively, you can simply sew a small two-hole button onto your piglet's face.

Use black yarn to embroider the eyes evenly on either side of the snout.

Size
Using the suggested yarn and hook, your sheep's body will be about (2in) 5cm long.

Actual size

You will need
Medium-weight yarn in main colour – approx 16½yd (15m)
Medium-weight yarn in contrast colour – approx 5½yd (5m)
Crochet hook – 3.5mm (UK9:USE/4)
Toy stuffing
Yarn needle
Craft felt in face colour
Embroidery needle
Embroidery thread in black
   and face colour

Abbreviations
See page 154

Sheep

Sheep are the woolliest of all the farm animals.
This little sheep has a crocheted body, hooves
and ears, with a felt face and embroidered
details. For extra woolliness, you can brush
out your sheep's body with a stiff-bristled
brush before adding the features.

BODY

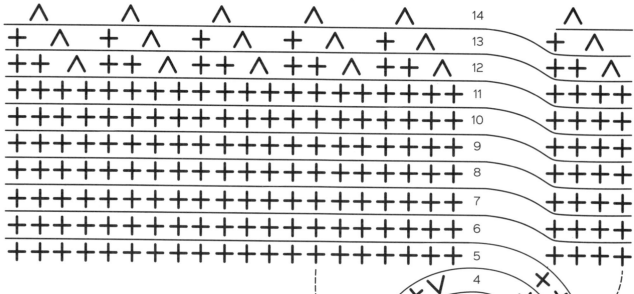

KEY

- •   start
- **O**   adjustable ring
- ⬭   chain
- ⬮   slip stitch
- **+**   double crochet
- **T**   half treble crochet
- **T̄**   treble crochet
- **V**   2 double crochet in 1 stitch
- **Λ**   double crochet 2 together

HOOVES

EARS

FACE TEMPLATE
100% SCALE

Body

The sheep's body is crocheted from back to front. Work in the round, without joining rounds. Using main colour, start with an adjustable ring.

1 6 dc into ring.
2 2 dc in each st around (12 dc).
3 (2 dc in next st, dc in next st) 6 times (18 dc).
4 (2 dc in next st, dc in next 2 sts) 6 times (24 dc).
5–11 Dc in each st around, for 7 rounds (24 dc per round).
12 (Dc2tog, dc in next 2 sts) 6 times (18 sts).
13 (Dc2tog, dc in next st) 6 times (12 sts).
Stuff the body, making it nice and puffy.
14 (Dc2tog) 6 times (6 sts).
Cut yarn, leaving a long tail for sewing, and finish off. Add a little more stuffing if necessary, then sew the hole closed.

Hooves

(make 4)
Using contrast colour, start with an adjustable ring.
1 6 dc into ring.
Cut yarn, leaving a long tail for sewing, and finish off. Join round.

Ears

(make 2)
Using contrast colour, chain 3.
1 Dc in the very first chain.
Cut yarn, leaving a long tail for sewing, and finish off.

Finishing

If you want your sheep to be extra-woolly, now is a good time to brush the yarn out with a stiff brush. Keep brushing until you have the desired amount of woolliness. This technique works best with wool or acrylic yarns, but may not work with cotton or cotton blends.

Sew the four hooves onto the bottom of your sheep. The back hooves should line up with rounds 5 and 6 of the body; the front hooves should line up with rounds 9 and 10. You can pin the hooves in place to make sure they are straight before sewing. Use the template to cut a face shape out of felt. Pin the face onto the front of your sheep, and sew in place using a matching colour thread.
Sew the ears in place, at the top corners of the face. Complete your sheep by using black thread to embroider two small eyes and a T-shape for a nose.

Pet Animals

Actual size

Size
Using the suggested yarn and hook, your bunny's body will be about 2in (5cm) tall.

You will need
Medium-weight yarn in main colour – approx 16½yd (15m)
Medium-weight yarn in contrast colour – approx 11yd (10m)
Medium-weight yarn in black – approx 1yd (1m)
Crochet hook – 3.5mm (UK9:USE/4)
Toy stuffing
Yarn needle
Embroidery needle
Embroidery thread in black

Abbreviations
See page 154

Bunny

Bunnies have a chubby body made from the top
down, with crocheted ears and paws sewn on.
A tail is added somewhere near the bottom.
Work with a single colour for a bare bunny, or
use two colours to make a pyjama-wearing bunny.
Bunny pyjamas are always tailored to fit.

BODY

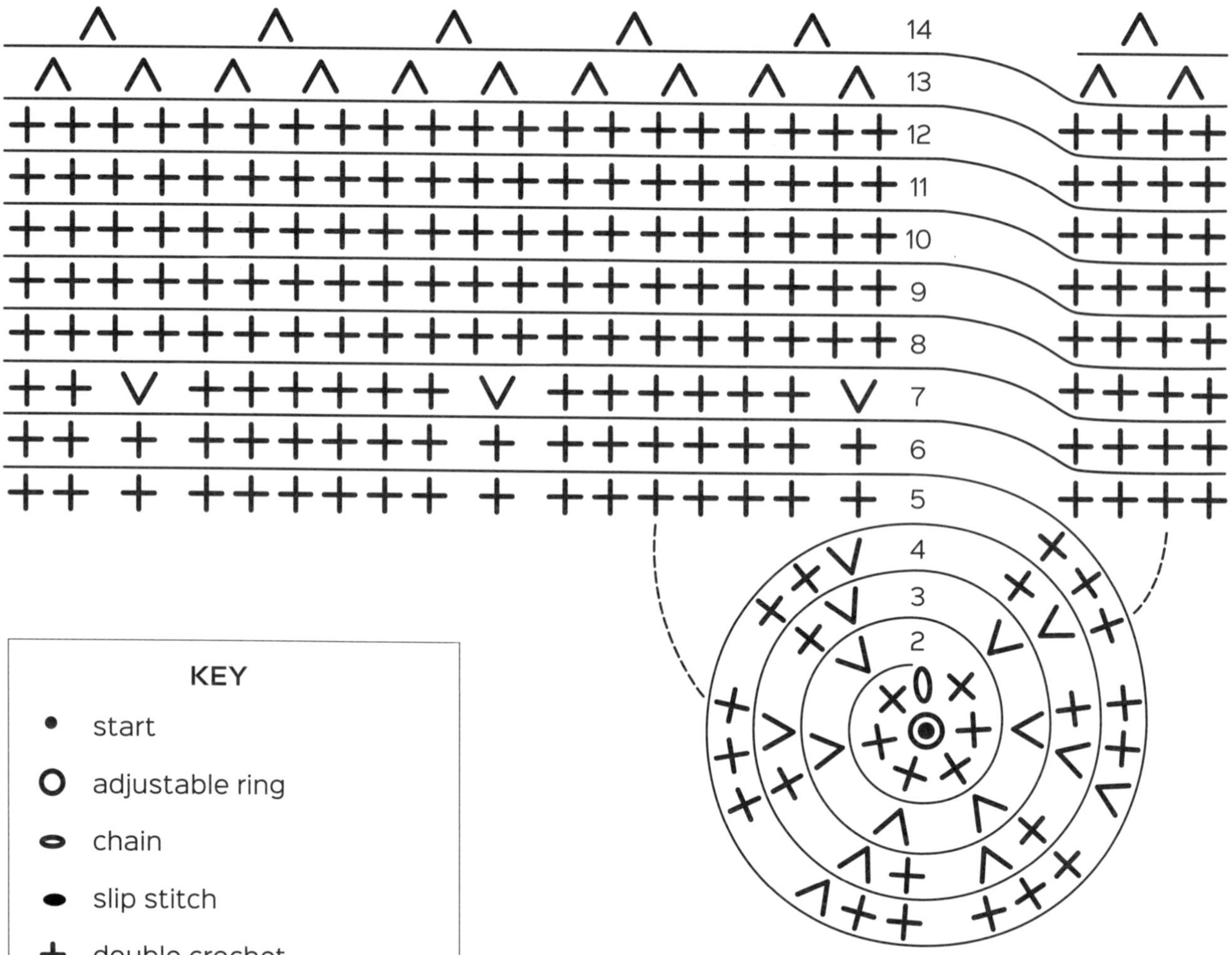
14
13
12
11
10
9
8
7
6
5
4
3
2

KEY

- • start
- O adjustable ring
- ⊖ chain
- ⬬ slip stitch
- + double crochet
- T half treble crochet
- Ŧ treble crochet
- V 2 double crochet in 1 stitch
- Λ double crochet 2 together

FEET & TAIL

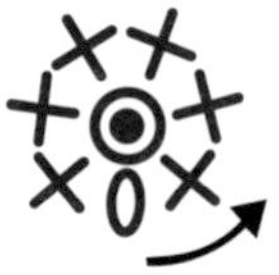

EARS

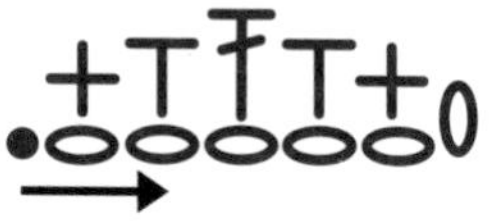

HANDS

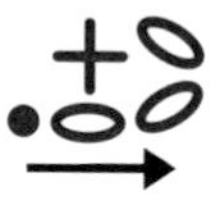

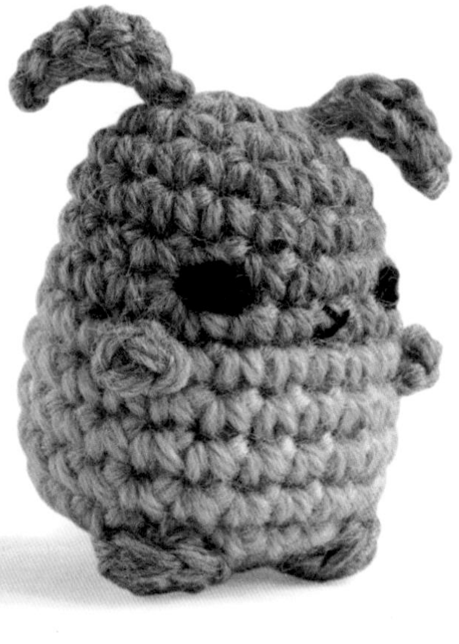

Body

The bunny's body is crocheted from top to bottom. Work in the round, without joining rounds. Using main colour, start with an adjustable ring.

1 6 dc into ring.

2 2 dc in each st around (12 dc).

3 (2 dc in next st, dc in next st) 6 times (18 dc).

4 (2 dc in next st, dc in next 5 sts) 3 times (21 dc).

5–6 Dc in each st around, for 2 rounds (21 dc per round).

7 (2 dc in next st, dc in next 6 sts) 3 times (24 dc).

If you're using two colours, change to the contrast colour now.

8–12 Dc in each st around, for 5 rounds (24 dc per round).

13 (Dc2tog) 12 times (12 sts). Stuff the body, making it nice and puffy.

14 (Dc2tog) 6 times (6 sts). Cut yarn, leaving a long tail for sewing, and finish off. Add a little more stuffing if necessary, then sew the hole closed.

Ears

(make 2)

Using main colour, ch 6.

1 Dc in 2nd ch from hook, htr in next ch, tr in next ch, htr in next ch, dc in last ch (5 sts).

Cut yarn, leaving a long tail for sewing, and finish off.

Hands

(make 2)

Using main colour, ch 3.

1 Dc in very first ch.

Cut yarn, leaving a long tail for sewing, and finish off.

Feet and tail

(make 3)

Using main colour, start with an adjustable ring.

1 6 dc into ring.

Cut yarn, leaving a long tail for sewing, and finish off. Join round.

Finishing

Use black yarn to embroider the eyes between rounds 6 and 7 of the body, about 3 stitches apart. For the mouth, use black thread to sew a small X-shape on round 7 of the body, in between the eyes.

Sew the ears onto the top of your bunny's head, between rounds 2 and 3.

Sew the hands in place. They should be between rounds 8 and 9 of the body, and about 4 stitches apart.

Sew the feet onto the front of your bunny, in line with rounds 12 and 13 of the body.

Finally, sew the tail onto the back of your bunny's body, more or less in line with the feet.

Actual size

Size

Using the suggested yarn and hook, your cat's body will be about 2in (5cm) tall.

You will need

Medium-weight yarn in main colour – approx 22yd (20m)
Medium-weight yarn in stripe colour – approx 1yd (1m)
Medium-weight yarn in black – approx 1yd (1m)
Crochet hook – 3.5mm (UK9:USE/4)
Toy stuffing
Yarn needle
Embroidery needle
Embroidery thread in black

Abbreviations

See page 154

Cat

This cat has a mostly round body, two crocheted
ears, four paws and a tail. The crocheted
details are sewn directly onto the cat,
along with an embroidered face and whiskers.
Different colours and stripes make different
cats, so you can crochet an amigurumi version
of your own cat friend.

BODY

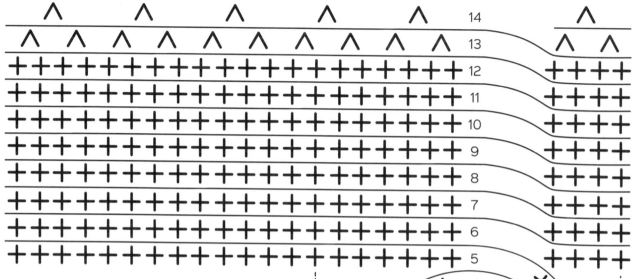

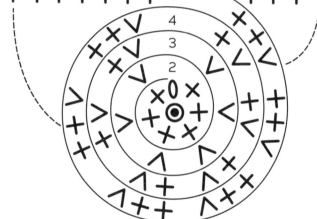

KEY

- **●** start
- **O** adjustable ring
- **⬮** chain
- **⬮** slip stitch
- **+** double crochet
- **T** half treble crochet
- **Ŧ** treble crochet
- **V** 2 double crochet in 1 stitch
- **∧** double crochet 2 together

TAIL

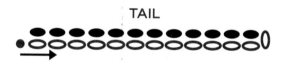

FEET

HANDS · EARS

Body

The cat's body is crocheted from top to bottom. Work in the round, without joining rounds.

Using main colour, start with an adjustable ring.

1 6 dc into ring.

2 2 dc in each st around (12 dc).

3 (2 dc in next st, dc in next st) 6 times (18 dc).

4 (2 dc in next st, dc in next 2 sts) 6 times (24 dc).

5–12 Dc in each st around, for 8 rounds (24 dc per round).

13 (Dc2tog) 12 times (12 sts). Stuff the body, making it nice and puffy.

14 (Dc2tog) 6 times (6 sts). Cut yarn, leaving a long tail for sewing, and finish off. Add a little more stuffing if necessary, then sew the hole closed.

Ears

(make 2)

Using main colour, ch 3.

1 Htr in the very first ch. Cut yarn, leaving a long tail for sewing, and finish off.

Hands

(make 2)

Using main colour, ch 3.

1 Dc in the very first ch. Cut yarn, leaving a long tail for sewing, and finish off.

Feet

(make 2)

Using main colour, start with an adjustable ring.

1 6 dc into ring. Cut yarn, leaving a long tail for sewing, and finish off. Join round.

Tail

Using main colour, ch 13.

1 Sl st in 2nd ch from hook, sl st in remaining 11 ch (12 sl st). Cut yarn, leaving a long tail for sewing, and finish off.

Finishing

Use black yarn to embroider the eyes between rounds 6 and 7 of the body, about 4 stitches apart. Use black thread to sew a small mouth and nose in between the eyes. Add some whiskers on either side of the eyes.

Sew the ears onto the top of your cat's head, in line with rounds 2 and 3 of the body.

Sew the hands in place just below the eyes. They should be in line with round 8 of the body, about 4 stitches apart.

Sew the feet onto the front of your cat, in line with rounds 11 and 12 of the body.

Sew the tail onto the back of the body, more or less in line with the feet.

Finally, use a matching yarn to sew three stripes onto the top of the head.

Actual size

Size

Using the suggested yarn and hook, your dog's body will be about 2in (5cm) long.

You will need

Medium-weight yarn in main colour – approx 16½yd (15m)
Medium-weight yarn in contrast colour – approx 5½yd (5m)
Medium-weight yarn in black – approx 1yd (1m)
Crochet hook – 3.5mm (UK9:USE/4)
Yarn needle
Toy stuffing

Abbreviations

See page 154

Dog

This dog's body is made back to front. The paws,
snout and ears are crocheted and sewn on.
The end result is a fairly pug-like dog, but
by changing the colours or other features
you could make a variety of dog friends.
This particular dog has no tail.

BODY

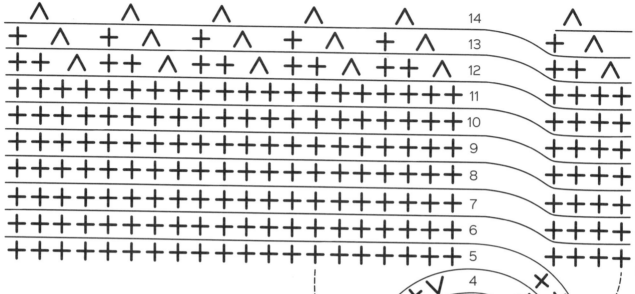

PAWS

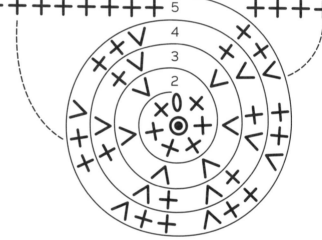

EARS

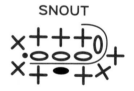

SNOUT

Body

The dog's body is crocheted from back to front. Work in the round, without joining rounds.
Using main colour, start with an adjustable ring.
1 6 dc into ring.
2 2 dc in each st around (12 dc).
3 (2 dc in next st, dc in next st) 6 times (18 dc).
4 (2 dc in next st, dc in next 2 sts) 6 times (24 dc).
5–11 Dc in each st around, for 7 rounds (24 dc per round).
12 (Dc2tog, dc in next 2 sts) 6 times (18 sts).
13 (Dc2tog, dc in next st) 6 times (12 sts).
Stuff the body, making it nice and puffy.
14 (Dc2tog) 6 times (6 sts).
Cut yarn, leaving a long tail for sewing, and finish off. Add a little more stuffing if necessary, then sew the hole closed.

Paws

(make 4)
Using main colour, start with an adjustable ring.
1 6 dc into ring.
Cut yarn, leaving a long tail for sewing, and finish off. Join round.

Snout

Using contrast colour, ch 4.
1 Dc in 2nd ch from hook, dc in next ch, 4 dc in last ch. Rotate your work so that you can crochet back down the bottom of the starting chain. Sl st in next ch, 3 dc in last ch.
Cut yarn, leaving a long tail for sewing, and finish off. Join round.

Ears

(make 2)
Using contrast colour, ch 4.
1 (Dc, ch 1) in 2nd ch from hook, (tr, ch 2) in next ch, sl st in last ch.
Cut yarn, leaving a tail for sewing, and finish off.

Finishing

Sew the four paws onto the bottom of your dog. The back paws should line up with rounds 5 and 6 of the body, and the front paws should line up with rounds 9 and 10. You can pin them in place to make sure they are straight before sewing.
Sew the snout in place, right in the middle of your dog's face.
Use black yarn to embroider the eyes evenly on either side of the snout.
Sew the ears in place, in line with rounds 9 and 10 of the body and about 6 stitches apart.

Size

Using the suggested yarn and hook, your fish's body will be about 2in (5cm) long.

Actual size

You will need

Medium-weight yarn in main colour – approx 22yd (20m)
Medium-weight yarn in white – approx 2yd (2m)
Medium-weight yarn in black – approx 1yd (1m)
Crochet hook – 3.5mm (UK9:USE/4)
Toy stuffing
Yarn needle
Embroidery needle
Embroidery thread in black

Abbreviations

See page 154

Goldfish

The goldfish has a simple squishy body, with a tail and fins that are crocheted before being carefully sewn on. Shiny or multicoloured yarns can be used to make it look shimmery, like a fish. This goldfish has unusually bulgy eyes.

BODY

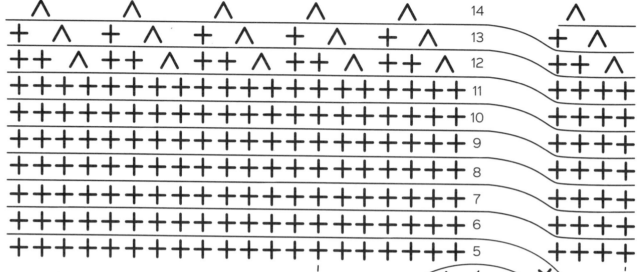

KEY

- **•** start
- **O** adjustable ring
- **⊖** chain
- **⬣** slip stitch
- **+** double crochet
- **T** half treble crochet
- **Ŧ** treble crochet
- **V** 2 double crochet in 1 stitch
- **∧** double crochet 2 together

TAIL

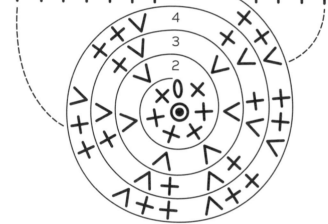

TOP FIN

SIDE FINS

EYES

Body

The goldfish body is crocheted from back to front. Work in the round, without joining rounds. Using main colour, start with an adjustable ring.

1 6 dc into ring.

2 2 dc in each st around (12 dc).

3 (2 dc in next st, dc in next st) 6 times (18 dc).

4 (2 dc in next st, dc in next 2 sts) 6 times (24 dc).

5–11 Dc in each st around, for 7 rounds (24 dc per round).

12 (Dc2tog, dc in next 2 sts) 6 times (18 sts).

13 (Dc2tog, dc in next st) 6 times (12 sts).
Stuff the body, making it nice and puffy.

14 (Dc2tog) 6 times (6 sts).
Cut yarn, leaving a long tail for sewing, and finish off. Add a little more stuffing if necessary, then sew the hole closed.

Tail

Using main colour, ch 8.

1 Tr in 4th ch from hook, htr in next ch, sl st in next ch, htr in next ch, tr in next ch, ch 2, sl st in same space as last tr st.
Cut yarn, leaving a long tail for sewing, and finish off.

Top fin

Using main colour, ch 6.

1 Tr in 3rd ch from hook, htr in next ch, dc in next ch, sl st in final ch.
Cut yarn, leaving a long tail for sewing, and finish off.

Side fins

(make 2)
Using main colour, ch 3.

1 Dc in very first ch.
Cut yarn, leaving a long tail for sewing, and finish off.

Eyes

(make 2)
Using white yarn, start with an adjustable ring and ch 2.

1 Ch 2, 8 htr into ring.
Cut yarn, leaving a long tail for sewing, and finish off. Join round.

Finishing

Sew the tail onto the back of your goldfish's body, right in the middle.
Sew the top fin on top, in line with rounds 7 to 10 of the body.
Sew the side fins onto the sides, in line with round 8 of the body.
Using black yarn, sew a pupil onto each bulgy eye.
Sew the eyes onto the front of the face.
Finally, use black thread to embroider a tiny mouth.

Actual size

Size

Using the suggested yarn and hook, your guinea pig's body will be about 2in (5cm) long.

You will need

Medium-weight yarn in main colour – approx 16½ yd (15m)
Medium-weight yarn in contrast colour – approx 5½yd (5m)
Medium-weight yarn in pink – approx 1yd (1m)
Crochet hook – 3.5mm (UK9:USE/4)
Toy stuffing
Yarn needle
Embroidery needle
Embroidery thread in black
Craft felt to match main colour
Embroidery thread to match craft felt

Abbreviations

See page 154

Guinea pig

Amigurumi guinea pig bodies are crocheted from
back to front, with a colour change along the
way. Crocheted paws and ears are sewn on, with
felt eye patches and embroidered face details.
Making custom varieties is easy if you use
different colours. You'll need at least two
guinea pigs to keep them from getting lonely.

BODY

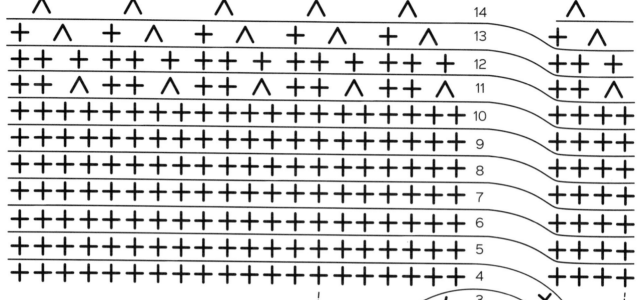

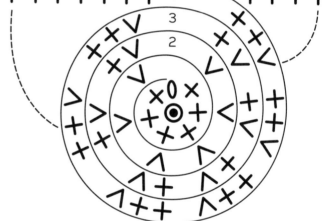

KEY

- **•** start
- **O** adjustable ring
- **⊶** chain
- **⊷** slip stitch
- **+** double crochet
- **T** half treble crochet
- **Ŧ** treble crochet
- **V** 2 double crochet in 1 stitch
- **Λ** double crochet 2 together

PAWS

EARS

EYE PATCH TEMPLATES 100% SCALE

Body

The guinea pig's body is crocheted from back to front. Work in the round, without joining rounds. Using main colour, start with an adjustable ring.

1 6 dc into ring.

2 2 dc in each st around (12 dc).

3 (2 dc in next st, dc in next st) 6 times (18 dc).

4 (2 dc in next st, dc in next 2 sts) 6 times (24 dc).

5–9 Dc in each st around, for 5 rounds (24 dc per round).

Change to contrast colour.

10–11 Dc in each st around, for 2 rounds (24 dc per round).

12 (Dc2tog, dc in next 2 sts) 6 times (18 sts).

13 Dc in each st around (18 dc).

14 (Dc2tog, dc in next st) 6 times (12 sts).

Stuff the body, making it nice and puffy.

15 (Dc2tog) 6 times (6 sts). Cut yarn, leaving a long tail for sewing, and finish off. Add a little more stuffing if necessary, then sew the hole closed.

Paws

(make 4)

Using main colour, start with an adjustable ring.

1 6 dc into ring.

Cut yarn, leaving a long tail for sewing, and finish off. Join round.

Ears

(make 2)

Using main colour, start with an adjustable ring.

1 (Dc, htr, tr, htr, dc) into ring (5 sts).

Do not join the round.

Cut yarn, leaving a long tail for sewing, and finish off.

Finishing

Sew the four paws onto the bottom of your guinea pig. The back paws should line up with rounds 5 and 6 of the body; the front paws should line up with rounds 9 and 10. You can pin them in place to make sure they are straight before sewing. Using the templates, cut two eye patch shapes out of felt. With matching thread, sew the felt shapes onto the face.

Use pink yarn to sew a nose in the middle of your guinea pig's face.

Use black thread to sew an eye onto each felt eye patch, roughly in line with the nose.

Finally, sew the ears in place. They should be in line with round 10 of the body, and about 6 stitches apart.

Sea Animals

Actual size

Size

Using the suggested yarn and hook, your penguin's body will be about 2in (5cm) tall.

You will need

Medium-weight yarn in black – approx 11yd (10m)
Medium-weight yarn in grey – approx 16½yd (15m)
Crochet hook – 3.5mm (UK9:USE/4)
Toy stuffing
Yarn needle
Craft felt in white
Embroidery needle
Embroidery thread in black, white and grey

Abbreviations

See page 154

Penguin

This small but versatile baby penguin is made
from the top down, with a colour change at
the neck. It has crocheted wings and a tail,
felt eye patches, and an embroidered face.
For an extra-fluffy penguin, brush out the
body before sewing on the details. The fluffier
the penguin, the warmer it will be.

BODY

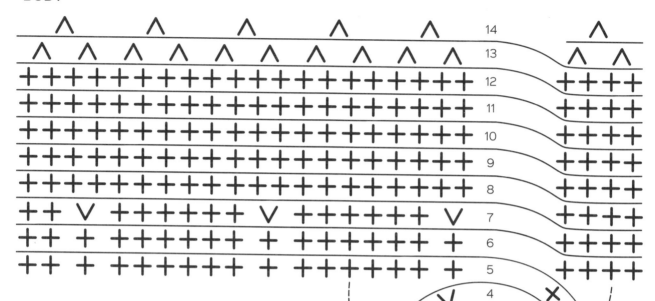

KEY

- **•** start
- **O** adjustable ring
- **⊙** chain
- **⬤** slip stitch
- **+** double crochet
- **T** half treble crochet
- **Ŧ** treble crochet
- **V** 2 double crochet in 1 stitch
- **∧** double crochet 2 together

WINGS

TAIL

EYE TEMPLATE 100% SCALE

Body

The penguin's body is crocheted from top to bottom. Work in the round, without joining rounds. Using black yarn, start with an adjustable ring.

1 6 dc into ring.

2 2 dc in each st around (12 dc).

3 (2 dc in next st, dc in next st) 6 times (18 dc).

4 (2 dc in next st, dc in next 5 sts) 3 times (21 dc).

5–6 Dc in each st around, for 2 rounds (21 dc per round).

7 (2 dc in next st, dc in next 6 sts) 3 times (24 dc). Change to grey yarn.

8–12 Dc in each st around, for 5 rounds (24 dc per round).

13 (Dc2tog) 12 times (12 sts). Stuff the body, making it nice and puffy.

14 (Dc2tog) 6 times (6 sts). Cut yarn, leaving a long tail for sewing, and finish off. Add a little more stuffing if necessary, then sew the hole closed.

Wings

(make 2)
Using grey yarn, start with an adjustable ring.

1 (Dc, htr, 2 tr, htr, dc) into ring (6 sts). Do not join round. Cut yarn, leaving a long tail for sewing, and finish off.

Tail

Using grey yarn, start with an adjustable ring.

1 4 dc into ring. Do not join round. Cut yarn, leaving a long tail for sewing, and finish off.

Finishing

If you are making a fluffy penguin, now is a good time to brush out the yarn on the body with a stiff brush. This works best with wool or acrylic yarns.

Using the template, cut two eye shapes out of white felt. Sew the shapes onto your penguin's head just above the colour change, about 3 stitches apart.

Use grey thread to embroider a small beak in between the eyes, in line with round 7 of the body. Use black thread to embroider an eye in the middle of each felt eye patch.

Sew the wings in place, between rounds 8 and 9 of the body and about 7 stitches apart.

Finally, sew the little tail onto the back of your penguin, between rounds 12 and 13 of the body.

Actual size

Size

Using the suggested yarn and hook, your otter's body will be about 2in (5cm) tall.

You will need

Medium-weight yarn in light brown – approx 11yd (10m)
Medium-weight yarn in dark brown – approx 16½yd (15m)
Medium-weight yarn in black – approx 1yd (1m)
Crochet hook – 3.5mm (UK9:USE/4)
Toy stuffing
Yarn needle
Craft felt in off-white
Embroidery needle
Embroidery thread in black and off-white

Abbreviations

See page 154

Otter

Otters have a relatively chunky body, small crocheted ears, four paws and a tail. A little felt snout is sewn onto the face, along with a nice embroidered nose and some well-placed whiskers. Amigurumi otters like to hold hands, and look extra-cute in pairs.

BODY

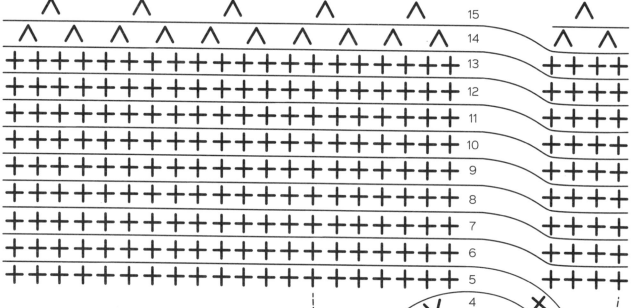

KEY

- **●** start
- **O** adjustable ring
- **⬮** chain
- **⬤** slip stich
- **+** double crochet
- **T** half treble crochet
- **Ŧ** treble crochet
- **V** 2 double crochet in 1 stich
- **∧** double crochet 2 together

FEET

EARS & HANDS

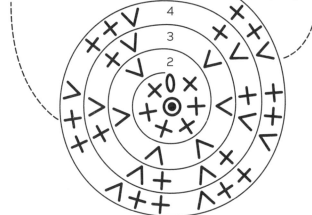

TAIL

SNOUT TEMPLATE 100% SCALE

Body

The otter's body is crocheted from top to bottom. Work in the round, without joining rounds. Using light brown yarn, start with an adjustable ring.

1 6 dc into ring.

2 2 dc in each st around (12 dc).

3 (2 dc in next st, dc in next st) 6 times (18 dc).

4 (2 dc in next st, dc in next 2 sts) 6 times (24 dc).

5–7 Dc in each st around, for 3 rounds (24 dc per round).

Change to dark brown yarn.

8–13 Dc in each st around, for 6 rounds (24 dc per round).

14 (Dc2tog) 12 times (12 sts). Stuff the body, making it nice and puffy.

15 (Dc2tog) 6 times (6 sts). Cut yarn, leaving a long tail for sewing, and finish off. Add a little more stuffing if necessary, then sew the hole closed.

Ears and hands

(make 4)

Using dark brown yarn, ch 3.

1 Dc in the very first ch. Cut yarn, leaving a long tail for sewing, and finish off.

Feet

(make 2)

Using dark brown yarn, start with an adjustable ring.

1 6 dc into ring. Cut yarn, leaving a long tail for sewing, and finish off. Join round.

Tail

Using light brown yarn, ch 8.

1 Sl st in 2nd ch from hook, dc in next 2 ch, htr in next 2 ch, tr in next 2 ch (7 sts). Cut yarn, leaving a long tail for sewing, and finish off.

Finishing

Use black yarn to embroider two eyes onto your otter's head, between rounds 6 and 7 of the body and about 4 stitches apart.

Using the template, cut one snout shape out of off-white felt.

Use off-white thread to sew the snout onto the front of your otter's face, in between the eyes.

Use black thread to embroider a mouth and nose onto the felt snout. Add a few small stitches for whiskers.

Sew the ears on top of the head, in line with round 3 of the body.

Sew the hands just below the eyes, in line with round 9 of the body and about 4 stitches apart.

Sew the feet in place, in line with rounds 12 and 13 of the body.

Sew the tail onto the back of your otter, so that it lines up with the top of the feet.

Actual size

Size
Using the suggested yarn and hook, your sea bunny's body will be about 2in (5cm) long.

You will need
Medium-weight yarn in main colour – approx 16½yd (15m)
Medium-weight yarn in black – approx 11yd (10m)
Crochet hook – 3.5mm (UK9:USE/4)
Toy stuffing
Yarn needle

Abbreviations
See page 154

Sea bunny

The sea bunny is not even a real bunny. Its
body starts as an oval, instead of the usual
circle shape. Then the tail and feelers are
crocheted and sewn on, and some embroidered
spots are added. Brush the body with a stiff
brush for an extra-fuzzy version. Making sea
bunnies is a good use of time on a sluggish day.

BODY

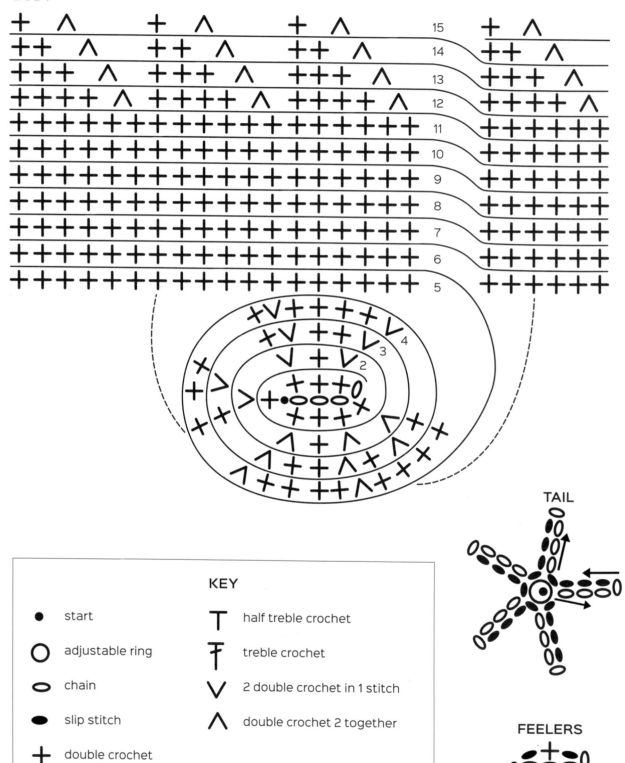

KEY

- ● start
- ◯ adjustable ring
- ◠ chain
- ⬮ slip stitch
- ✛ double crochet
- T half treble crochet
- Ŧ treble crochet
- V 2 double crochet in 1 stitch
- ∧ double crochet 2 together

TAIL

FEELERS

Body

The sea bunny's body is crocheted from back to front. Work in the round, without joining rounds. Using main colour yarn, ch 4.

1 Dc in 2nd ch from hook, dc in next ch, 3 dc in last ch. Rotate your work so that you can crochet back down the bottom of the starting chain. Dc in next ch, 2 dc in last ch (8 dc).

2 2 dc in the very first st of round 1, dc in next st, 2 dc in each of the next 3 sts, dc in next st, 2 dc in each of the next 2 sts (14 dc).

3 2 dc in next st, dc in next st, dc in next st, (2 dc in next st, dc in next st) 3 times, dc in next st, (2 dc in next st, dc in next st) twice (20 dc).

4 (2 dc in next st, dc in next 4 sts) 4 times (24 dc).

5–11 Dc in each st around, for 7 rounds (24 dc per round).

12 (Dc2tog, dc in next 4 sts) 4 times (20 sts).

13 (Dc2tog, dc in next 3 sts) 4 times (16 sts).

14 (Dc2tog, dc in next 2 sts) 4 times (12 sts).
Stuff the body, making it nice and puffy.

15 (Dc2tog, dc in next st) 4 times (8 sts).
Cut yarn, leaving a tail for sewing, and finish off. Add a little more stuffing if necessary, then sew the hole closed.

Feelers

(make 2)
Using black yarn, ch 4.

1 Sl st in 2nd ch from hook, dc in next ch, sl st in final ch (3 sts).
Cut yarn, leaving a long tail for sewing, and finish off.

Tail

Using black yarn, start with an adjustable ring.

1 (Ch 4, sl st in 2nd ch from hook, sl st in next 2 ch, sl st into ring) 5 times. After tightening the adjustable ring, you should have a shape that looks a bit like a starfish. Cut yarn, leaving a long tail for sewing, and finish off. Join round.

Finishing

Squash the body a little so that it has a slightly flat shape.
If you are making an extra-fuzzy sea bunny, brush the body with a stiff brush until you have the desired amount of fuzziness.
Use black yarn to sew the eyes onto the face, between rounds 13 and 14 of the body.
Sew a small black mouth in between the eyes.
To make the sea bunny's spots, use black yarn to make small stitches at random intervals all over the body.
Sew the feelers on top of your sea bunny's head, between rounds 11 and 12 of the body and about 3 stitches apart.
Finally, sew the tail onto the back of the body, so that the fronds stick up in the air.

Actual size

Size

Using the suggested yarn and hook, your seal's body will be about 2in (5cm) long.

You will need

Medium-weight yarn in main colour – approx 22yd (20m)
Medium-weight yarn in black – approx 1yd (1m)
Crochet hook – 3.5mm (UK9:USE/4)
Toy stuffing
Yarn needle

Abbreviations

See page 154

Seal

This seal starts off with a small loaf-shaped body. The snout, flippers and tail are crocheted and sewn on next. Complete your amigurumi by adding a cute little face. Baby seals like to be made of white yarn, especially when brushed out and extra-fluffy. Older seals are grey and not as fluffy.

BODY

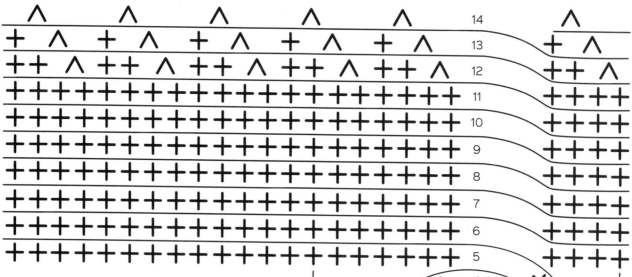

TAIL

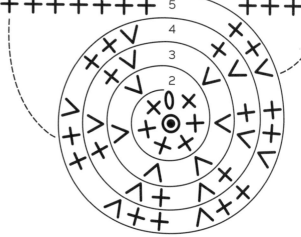

KEY

- **•** start
- **O** adjustable ring
- **⬭** chain
- **⬬** slip stitch
- **+** double crochet
- **T** half treble crochet
- **Ŧ** treble crochet
- **V** 2 double crochet in 1 stitch
- **Λ** double crochet 2 together

SNOUT

FLIPPERS

Flippers

(make 2)

Using main colour, start with an adjustable ring.
1 (Dc, htr, tr, htr, dc) into ring (5 sts).
Do not join round. Cut yarn, leaving a long tail for sewing, and finish off.

Tail

Using main colour, ch 8.
1 Tr in 4th ch from hook, htr in next ch, sl st in next ch, htr in next ch, tr in next ch, ch 2, sl st in same space as last tr st.
Cut yarn, leaving a long tail for sewing, and finish off.

Body

The seal's body is crocheted from back to front. Work in the round, without joining rounds. Using main colour, start with an adjustable ring.
1 6 dc into ring.
2 2 dc in each st around (12 dc).
3 (2 dc in next st, dc in next st) 6 times (18 dc).
4 (2 dc in next st, dc in next 2 sts) 6 times (24 dc).
5–11 Dc in each st around, for 7 rounds (24 dc per round).
12 (Dc2tog, dc in next 2 sts) 6 times (18 sts).
13 (Dc2tog, dc in next st) 6 times (12 sts).
Stuff the body, making it nice and puffy.

14 (Dc2tog) 6 times (6 sts).
Cut yarn, leaving a long tail for sewing, and finish off. Add a little more stuffing if necessary, then sew the hole closed.

Snout

Using main colour, ch 4.
1 Dc in 2nd ch from hook, dc in next ch, 4 dc in last ch. Rotate your work so that you can crochet back down the bottom of the starting chain. Sl st in next ch, 3 dc in last ch.
Cut yarn, leaving a long tail for sewing, and finish off. Join round.

Finishing

If you are making a fluffy baby seal, brush the body out with a stiff brush to make it extra-fuzzy.
Sew the snout onto your seal's face. The top of the snout should sit just above the middle of the face.
Using black yarn, sew the eyes on either side of the snout, between rounds 12 and 13 of the body.
Embroider a black nose onto the snout.
Sew the flippers onto the sides of your seal, in line with rounds 9 and 10 of the body.
Finally, sew the tail onto the back of the body, right in the middle.

Actual size

Size

Using the suggested yarn and hook, your whale's body will be about 2in (5cm) long.

You will need

Medium-weight yarn in main colour – approx 16½yd (15m)
Medium-weight yarn in white – approx 11yd (10m)
Medium-weight yarn in black – approx 1yd (1m)
Crochet hook – 3.5mm (UK9:USE/4)
Toy stuffing
Yarn needle

Abbreviations

See page 154

Whale

The amigurumi whale is crocheted from the top down, starting with an oval shape. A different colour is used to make its whale-like belly. The tail and fins are crocheted and sewn on, and the eyes are embroidered onto the head. This whale's body is significantly smaller than that of an average whale.

BODY

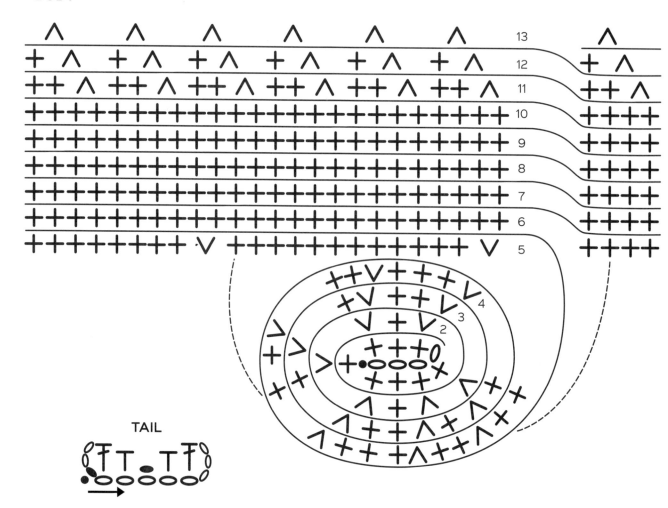

TAIL

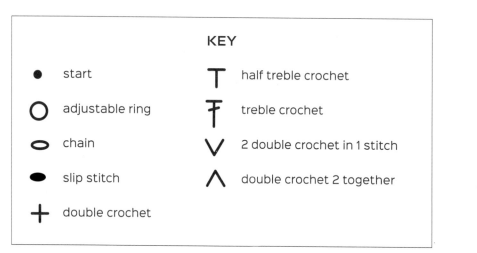

KEY

- ● start
- ○ adjustable ring
- ⬭ chain
- ⬤ slip stitch
- + double crochet

- T half treble crochet
- ‡ treble crochet
- V 2 double crochet in 1 stitch
- Λ double crochet 2 together

SIDE FINS

TOP FIN

Body

The whale's body is crocheted from top to bottom. Work in the round, without joining rounds. Using main colour yarn, ch 4.

1 Dc in 2nd ch from hook, dc in next ch, 3 dc in last ch. Rotate your work so that you can crochet back down the bottom of the starting chain. Dc in next ch, 2 dc in last ch (8 dc).

2 2 dc in the very first st of round 1, dc in next st, 2 dc in each of next 3 sts, dc in next st, 2 dc in each of next 2 sts (14 dc).

3 2 dc in next st, dc in next st, dc in next st, (2 dc in next st, dc in next st) 3 times, dc in next st, (2 dc in next st, dc in next st) twice (20 dc).

4 2 dc in next st, dc in next 2 sts, dc in next st, (2 dc in next st, dc in next 2 sts) 3 times, dc in next st, (2 dc in next st, dc in next 2 sts) twice (26 dc).

5 (2 dc in next st, dc in next 12 sts) twice (28 dc).

6–8 Dc in each st around, for 3 rounds (28 dc per round).

Change to white yarn.

9–10 Dc in each st around, for 2 rounds (28 dc per round).

11 (Dc2tog, dc in next 2 sts) 7 times (21 sts).

12 (Dc2tog, dc in next st) 7 times (14 sts).

Stuff the body, making it nice and puffy.

13 (Dc2tog) 7 times (7 sts). Cut the yarn, leaving a long tail for sewing, and finish off. Add a little more stuffing if necessary, then sew the hole closed.

Tail

Using main colour, ch 8.

1 Tr in 4th ch from hook, htr in next ch, sl st in next ch, htr in next ch, tr in next ch, ch 2, sl st in same space as last tr st.

Cut yarn, leaving a long tail for sewing, and finish off.

Side fins

(make 2)

Using main colour, start with an adjustable ring.

1 (Dc, htr, tr, htr, dc) into ring (5 sts).

Do not join round. Cut yarn, leaving a long tail for sewing, and finish off.

Top fin

Using main colour, ch 4.

1 Tr in the very first ch.

Cut yarn, leaving a long tail for sewing, and finish off.

Finishing

Locate the point on the whale's body where you changed from the main colour to white – this will be the tail end of your whale. Sew the tail on between rounds 8 and 9 of the body, using it to hide the colour change.

Use black yarn to sew the eyes onto the front of your whale. They should be between rounds 8 and 9 of the body, and about 5 stitches apart.

Sew the side fins in place, next to the eyes.

Sew the top fin onto your whale's back, with the treble stitch lying flat against the body. The top fin should be in line with rounds 2 to 4 of your whale's body.

Little Animals

Actual size

Size

Using the suggested yarn and hook, your butterfly's body will be about 2in (5cm) long.

You will need

Medium-weight yarn in body colour – approx 16½yd (15m)
Medium-weight yarn in face colour – approx 11yd (10m)
Medium-weight yarn in wing colour – approx 11yd (10m)
Medium-weight yarn in black – approx 1yd (1m)
Crochet hook – 3.5mm (UK9:USE/4)
Toy stuffing
Yarn needle
Embroidery needle
Embroidery thread in black

Abbreviations

See page 154

Butterfly

The butterfly is the most colourful amigurumi
creature. Its body is shaped like a small
loaf of bread. It has crocheted wings, feelers
and an embroidered face. Butterflies can be
made in all sorts of colour combinations - you
could even use multicoloured yarn if you are
feeling adventurous.

BODY

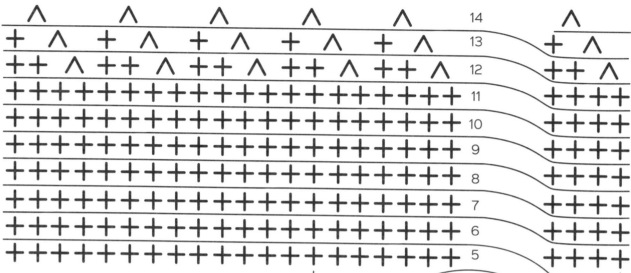

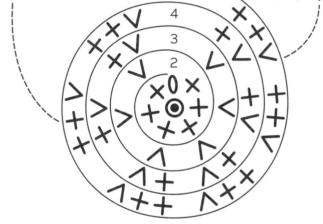

KEY

- **•** start
- **O** adjustable ring
- **⊝** chain
- **⬬** slip stitch
- **+** double crochet
- **T** half treble crochet
- **Ŧ** treble crochet
- **V** 2 double crochet in 1 stitch
- **∧** double crochet 2 together

LARGE WINGS

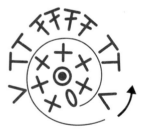

SMALL WINGS

FEELERS

Body

The butterfly's body is crocheted from back to front. Work in the round, without joining rounds. Using body colour, start with an adjustable ring.

1 6 dc into ring.

2 2 dc in each st around (12 dc).

3 (2 dc in next st, dc in next st) 6 times (18 dc).

4 (2 dc in next st, dc in next 2 sts) 6 times (24 dc).

5–9 Dc in each st around, for 5 rounds (24 dc per round).

Change to face colour.

10–11 Dc in each st around, for 2 rounds (24 dc per round).

12 (Dc2tog, dc in next 2 sts) 6 times (18 sts).

13 (Dc2tog, dc in next st) 6 times (12 sts).

Stuff the body, making it nice and puffy.

14 (Dc2tog) 6 times (6 sts).

Cut yarn, leaving a long tail for sewing, and finish off. Add a little more stuffing if necessary, then sew the hole closed.

Large wings

(make 2)

Using wing colour, start with an adjustable ring

1 6 dc into ring.

2 2 dc in next st, 2 htr in next st, 4 tr in next st, 2 htr in next st, 2 dc in next st (12 sts).

Do not join round. Cut yarn, leaving a long tail for sewing, and finish off.

Small wings

(make 2)

Using main colour, start with an adjustable ring.

1 (Dc, htr, 2 tr, htr, dc) into ring (6 sts).

Do not join round. Cut yarn, leaving a long tail for sewing, and finish off.

Feelers

(make 2)

Using body colour, ch 3.

1 Sl st in 2nd ch from hook, sl st in next ch.

Cut yarn, leaving a long tail for sewing, and finish off.

Finishing

With black yarn, sew two eyes onto your butterfly's face, in line with round 12 of the body.

Use black thread to sew a tiny mouth in between the eyes.

Sew the two large wings onto your butterfly, in line with rounds 7 to 9 of the body and about 4 stitches apart.

Sew the two small wings in place behind the large wings, in line with rounds 5 and 6 of the body.

Attach the feelers on top of the head, between rounds 10 and 11 of the body and about 6 stitches apart.

Actual size

Size

Using the suggested yarn and hook, your caterpillar's body will be about 1½in (4cm) wide.

You will need

Medium-weight yarn in main colour – approx 16 ½yd (15m)
Medium-weight yarn in contrast colour – approx 11yd (10m)
Medium-weight yarn in black – approx 1yd (1m)
Crochet hook – 3.5mm (UK9/USE/4)
Toy stuffing
Yarn needle
Embroidery needle
Embroidery thread in black

Abbreviations

See page 154

Caterpillar

Caterpillars are the longest of all the amigurumi creatures. Colour changes are used on the body to make their stripes. Although instructions are given for the shortest caterpillar, you can keep adding stripes to make the body as long as you want. Longer caterpillars will also require more legs.

BODY

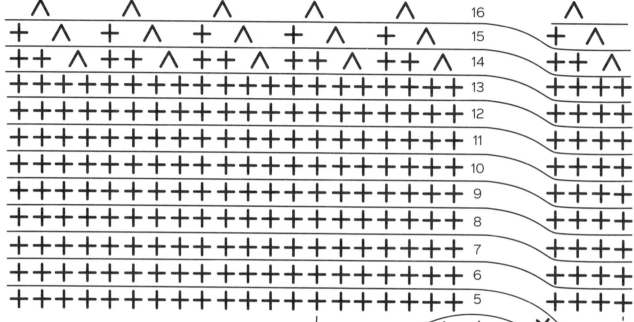

KEY

- **•** start
- **O** adjustable ring
- **⬭** chain
- **⬬** slip stitch
- **+** double crochet
- **T** half treble crochet
- **Ŧ** treble crochet
- **V** 2 double crochet in 1 stitch
- **Λ** double crochet 2 together

FEELERS & LEGS

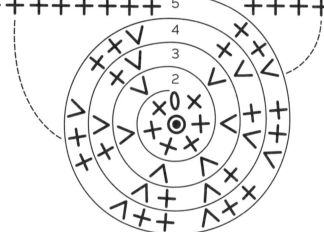

Body

The caterpillar's body is crocheted from back to front. Work in the round, without joining rounds. Using main colour, start with an adjustable ring.

1 6 dc into ring.

2 2 dc in each st around (12 dc).

3 (2 dc in next st, dc in next st) 6 times (18 dc).

4 (2 dc in next st, dc in next 2 sts) 6 times (24 dc).

5 Dc in each st around (24 dc).

Change to contrast colour.

6–7 Dc in each st around, for 2 rounds (24 dc per round).

Change to main colour.

8–9 Dc in each st around, for 2 rounds (24 dc per round).

Change to contrast colour.

10–11 Dc in each st around, for 2 rounds (24 dc per round).

To make a longer caterpillar, continue adding two rounds of each colour until you have the desired number of stripes.

End with a contrast colour stripe before continuing with the pattern.

Change to main colour.

12–13 Dc in each st around, for 2 rounds (24 dc per round).

14 (Dc2tog, dc in next 2 sts) 6 times (18 sts).

15 (Dc2tog, dc in next st) 6 times (12 sts).

Stuff the body, making it nice and puffy.

16 (Dc2tog) 6 times (6 sts).

Cut yarn, leaving a long tail for sewing, and finish off. Add a little morestuffing if necessary, then sew the hole closed.

Feelers and legs

(make 8)

Using contrast colour, ch 3.

1 Sl st in 2nd ch from hook, sl st in next ch.

Cut yarn, leaving a long tail for sewing, and finish off.

Finishing

With black yarn, embroider two eyes onto your caterpillar's face, in line with round 14 of the body. Use black thread to sew a small mouth in between the eyes.

Sew the feelers on top of the head between rounds 12 and 13 of the body, about 6 stitches apart.

Sew the legs onto your caterpillar's body, in line with the stripes. If you added more stripes to make a longer caterpillar, you will need to add more legs, too.

Actual size

Size

Using the suggested yarn and hook, your honey bee's body will be about 2½in (6cm) long.

You will need

Medium-weight yarn in yellow – approx 16½yd (15m)
Medium-weight yarn in black – approx 11yd (10m)
Medium-weight yarn in white – approx 2yd (2m)
Crochet hook – 3.5mm (UK9/USE/4)
Toy stuffing
Yarn needle
Embroidery needle
Embroidery thread in black

Abbreviations

See page 154

Honey bee

This mini honey bee is a sweet little amigurumi creature. It is crocheted from back to front, starting with the tiny stinger. An embroidered face, crocheted wings and legs are sewn on next. Bees are quite quick to crochet, and can look cute both with or without legs.

BODY

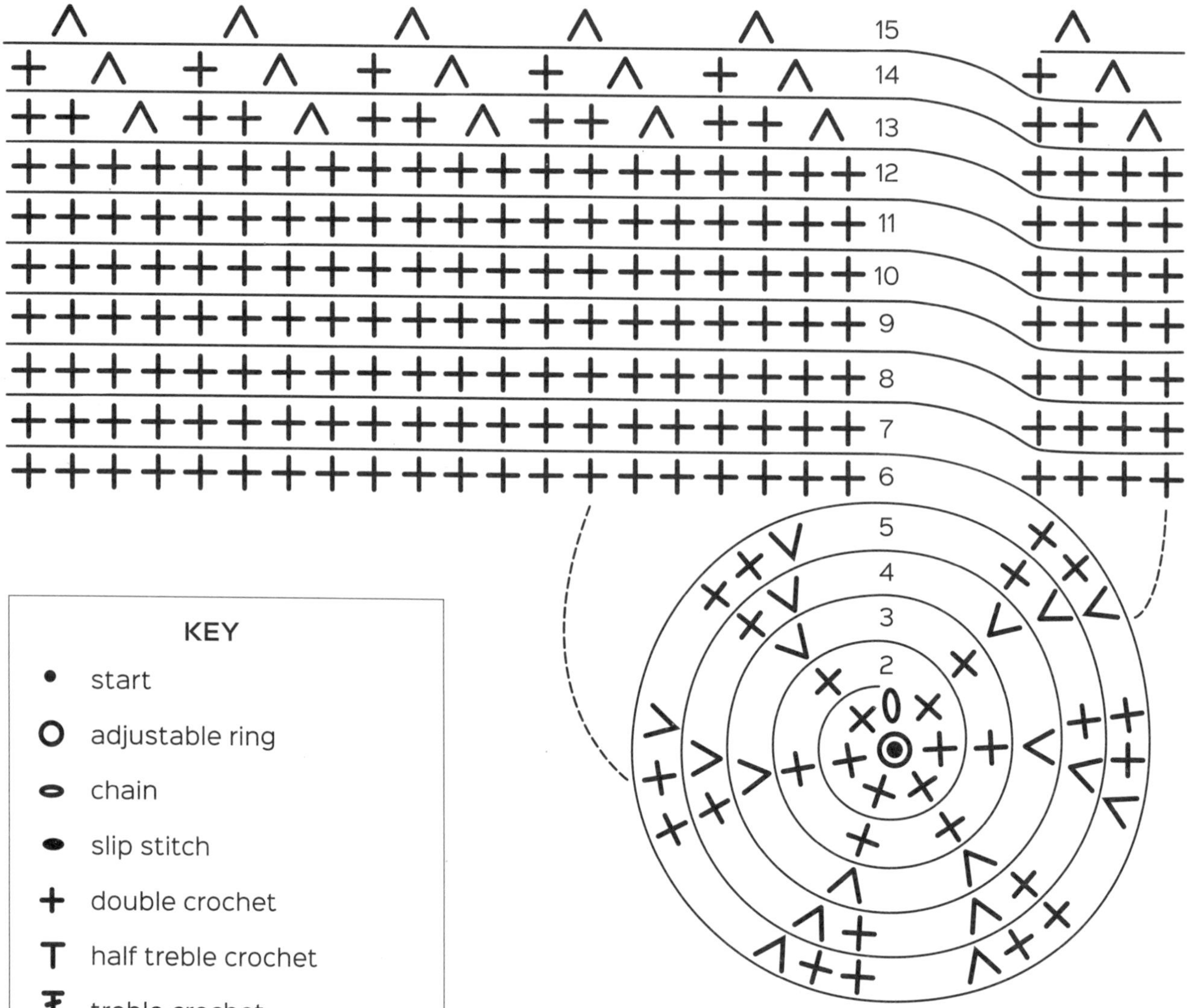

KEY	
•	start
O	adjustable ring
o	chain
●	slip stitch
+	double crochet
T	half treble crochet
Ŧ	treble crochet
V	2 double crochet in 1 stitch
Λ	double crochet 2 together

WINGS

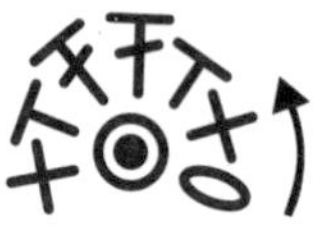

LEGS

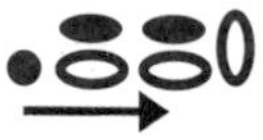

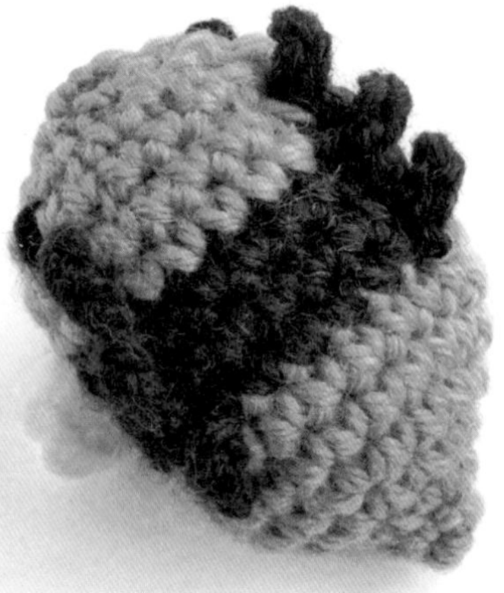

Body

The honey bee's body is crocheted from back to front. Work in the round, without joining rounds. Using yellow yarn, start with an adjustable ring.

1 6 dc into ring.

2 Dc in each st around (6 dc).

3 2 dc in each st around (12 dc).

4 (2 dc in next st, dc in next st) 6 times (18 dc).

5 (2 dc in next st, dc in next 2 sts) 6 times (24 dc).

6–7 Dc in each st around, for 2 rounds (24 dc per round).

Change to black yarn.

8–10 Dc in each st around, for 3 rounds (24 dc per round).

Change to yellow yarn.

11–12 Dc in each st around, for 2 rounds (24 dc per round).

13 (Dc2tog, dc in next 2 sts) 6 times (18 sts).

14 (Dc2tog, dc in next st) 6 times (12 sts).

Stuff the body, making it nice and puffy.

15 (Dc2tog) 6 times (6 sts).

Cut yarn, leaving a long tail for sewing, and finish off. Add a little more stuffing if necessary, then sew the hole closed.

Wings

(make 2)

Using white yarn, start with an adjustable ring.

1 (Dc, htr, 2 tr, htr, dc) into ring (6 sts).

Do not join the round. Cut the yarn, leaving a long tail for sewing, and finish off.

Legs

(make 6)

Using black yarn, chain 3.

1 Sl st in 2nd ch from hook, sl st in next ch.

Cut yarn, leaving a long tail for sewing, and finish off.

Finishing

Use black yarn to embroider two eyes onto your bee's face, in line with round 13 of the body. Use black thread to sew a small mouth in between the eyes.

Sew the wings onto your bee's back, in line with the black stripe and about 4 stitches apart.

Sew the legs in place, spacing them evenly on either side of the body.

Size

Using the suggested yarn and hook, your ladybird's body will be about 2in (5cm) long.

Actual size

You will need

Medium-weight yarn in red – approx 16½yd (15m)
Medium-weight yarn in brown – approx 11yd (10m)
Medium-weight yarn in black – approx 1yd (1m)
Crochet hook – 3.5mm (UK9:USE/4)
Toy stuffing
Yarn needle
Craft felt in black
Embroidery needle
Embroidery thread in black

Abbreviations

See page 154

Ladybird

A little ladybird will make a cute addition to your amigurumi insect collection. This creature has a small oval body with some felt spots sewn on, and a brown crocheted face and feelers. Although ladybirds are commonly found in red, yellow and orange specimens have also been known to appear.

BODY

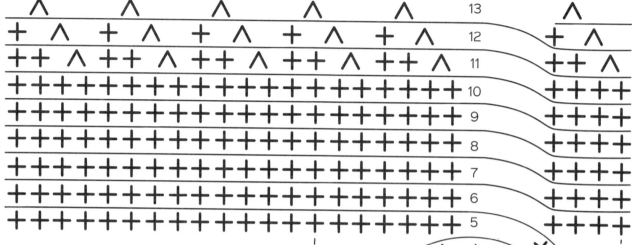

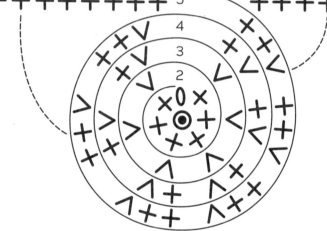

KEY

- **•** start
- **O** adjustable ring
- **◔** chain
- **◕** slip stitch
- **+** double crochet
- **T** half treble crochet
- **Ŧ** treble crochet
- **V** 2 double crochet in 1 stitch
- **Λ** double crochet 2 together

FACE

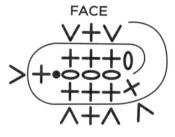

FEELERS

Body

The ladybird's body is crocheted from back to front. Work in the round, without joining rounds. Using red yarn, start with an adjustable ring.

1 6 dc into ring.

2 2 dc in each st around (12 dc).

3 (2 dc in next st, dc in next st) 6 times (18 dc).

4 (2 dc in next st, dc in next 2 sts) 6 times (24 dc).

5–10 Dc in each st around, for 6 rounds (24 dc per round).

11 (Dc2tog, dc in next 2 sts) 6 times (18 sts).

12 (Dc2tog, dc in next st) 6 times (12 sts). Stuff the body, making it nice and puffy.

13 (Dc2tog) 6 times (6 sts). Cut yarn, leaving a long tail for sewing, and finish off. Add a little more stuffing if necessary, then sew the hole closed.

Face

Using brown yarn, ch 4.

1 Dc in 2nd ch from hook, dc in next ch, 3 dc in last ch. Rotate your work so that you can crochet back down the bottom of the starting chain. Dc in next ch, 2 dc in last ch (8 dc).

2 2 dc in first st of round 1, dc in next st, 2 dc in each of next 3 sts, dc in next st, 2 dc in each of next 2 sts (14 dc).

Cut yarn, leaving a long tail for sewing, and finish off. Join round.

Feelers

(make 2)

Using brown yarn, chain 3.

1 Sl st in 2nd ch from hook, sl st in next ch.

Cut yarn, leaving a long tail for sewing, and finish off.

Finishing

Use black yarn to embroider two eyes onto your ladybird's face, in line with round 2 of the face. Use black thread to sew a small mouth in between the eyes.

Sew the face onto the front of your ladybird's body. Sew the feelers onto either side of the face.

To make a felt spot, first cut a ⅜in (1cm) square out of black craft felt. Cut away the corners of the square until you have a small circle. Make six little spots, and sew them onto the top of your ladybird's body.

Actual size

Size

Using the suggested yarn and hook, your snail's body will be about 2in (5cm) long.

You will need

Medium-weight yarn in body colour – approx 16½yd (15m)
Medium-weight yarn in shell colour – approx 11yd (10m)
Medium-weight yarn in black – approx 1yd (1m)
Crochet hook – 3.5mm (UK9:USE/4)
Toy stuffing
Yarn needle
Embroidery needle
Embroidery thread in black

Abbreviations

See page 154

Snail

This anatomically incorrect snail has
a squishy body, tiny feelers and a face.
The helmet-like shell is crocheted separately
and sewn on top. You can use multicoloured
yarn to make your snail's shell look more
interesting, or discard the shell altogether
to make a little amigurumi slug.

BODY

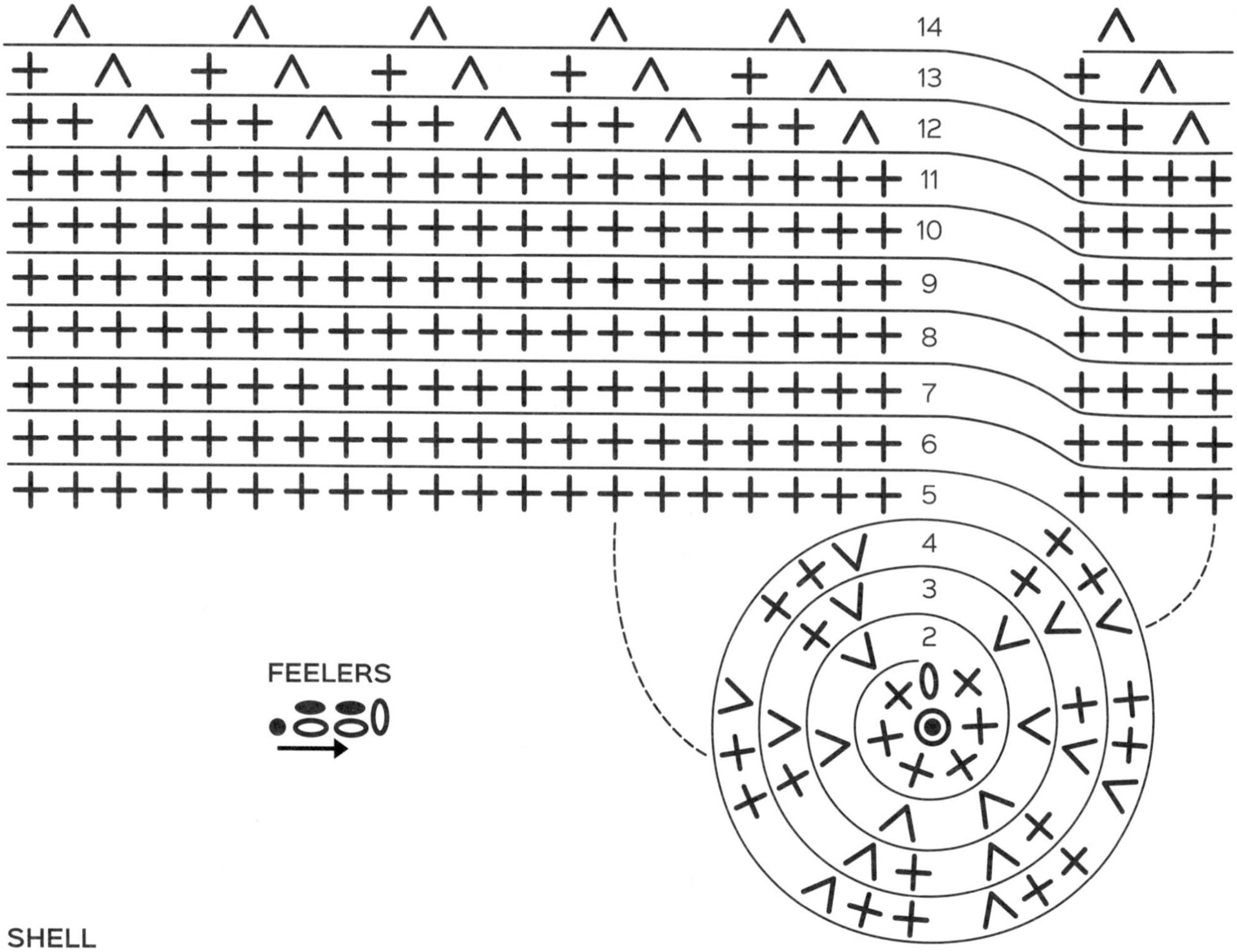

FEELERS

SHELL

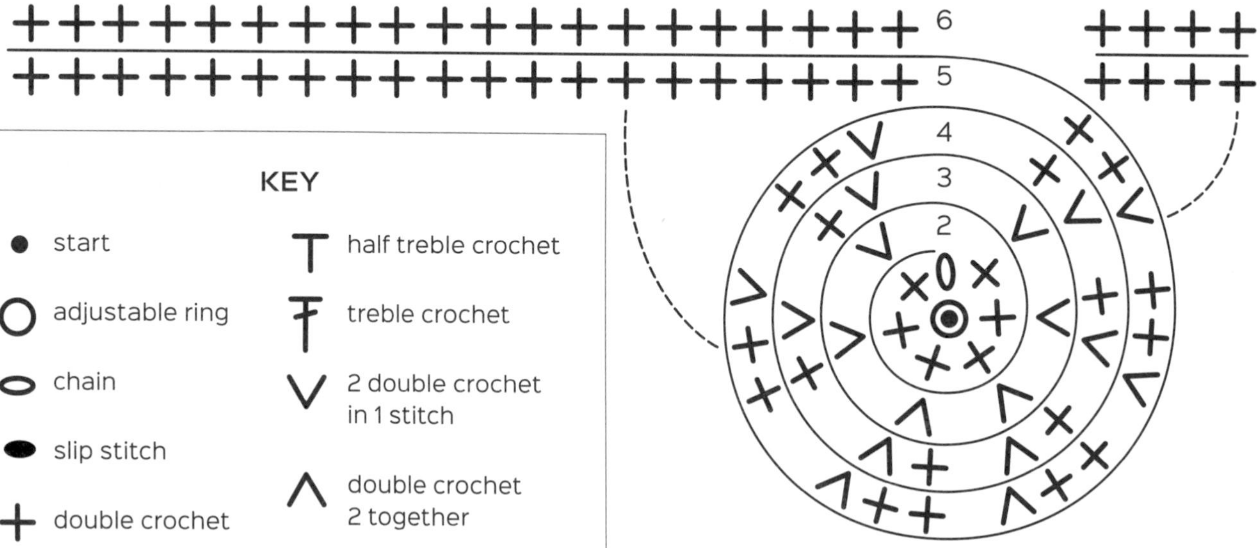

KEY

- ● start
- ○ adjustable ring
- chain
- slip stitch
- \+ double crochet
- half treble crochet
- treble crochet
- V 2 double crochet in 1 stitch
- Λ double crochet 2 together

Body

The snail's body is crocheted from back to front. Work in the round, without joining rounds. Using body colour, start with an adjustable ring.

1 6 dc into ring.

2 2 dc in each st around (12 dc).

3 (2 dc in next st, dc in next st) 6 times (18 dc).

4 (2 dc in next st, dc in next 2 sts) 6 times (24 dc).

5–11 Dc in each st around, for 7 rounds (24 dc per round).

12 (Dc2tog, dc in next 2 sts) 6 times (18 sts).

13 (Dc2tog, dc in next st) 6 times (12 sts).

Stuff the body, making it nice and puffy.

14 (Dc2tog) 6 times (6 sts).

Cut yarn, leaving a long tail for sewing, and finish off. Add a little more stuffing if necessary, then sew the hole closed.

Feelers

(make 2)

Using body colour, ch 3.

1 Sl st in 2nd ch from hook, sl st in next ch.

Cut yarn, leaving a long tail for sewing, and finish off.

Shell

Using shell colour, start with an adjustable ring.

1 6 dc into ring.

2 2 dc in each st around (12 dc).

3 (2 dc in next st, dc in next st) 6 times (18 dc).

4 (2 dc in next st, dc in next 2 sts) 6 times (24 dc).

5–6 Dc in each st around, for 2 rounds (24 dc per round).

Cut yarn, leaving a long tail for sewing, and finish off. Join round.

Finishing

Use black yarn to embroider two eyes onto your snail's face, in line with round 12 of the body. Use black thread to sew a small mouth in between the eyes.

Sew the feelers onto the head, between rounds 11 and 12 of the body and about 5 stitches apart. Position the shell on top of the snail's body, and start sewing it in place. Add some stuffing before closing the gap between the shell and body.

Woodland Animals

Actual size

Size
Using the suggested yarn
and hook, your bear's body
will be about 2in (5cm) tall.

You will need
Medium-weight yarn in body colour – approx 16½yd (15m)
Medium-weight yarn in pyjama colour – approx 16½yd (15m)
Medium-weight yarn in black – approx 1yd (1m)
Crochet hook – 3.5mm (UK9:USE/4)
Yarn needle
Toy stuffing
Craft felt in off-white
Embroidery needle
Embroidery thread in black and off-white

Abbreviations
See page 154

Bear

These bears are crocheted from the top down, with a colour change to give them some pyjamas. They have crocheted paws, ears and tails, along with felt snouts and embroidered eyes. If your bear does not enjoy wearing pyjamas, it can be made all in one single colour, too.

BODY

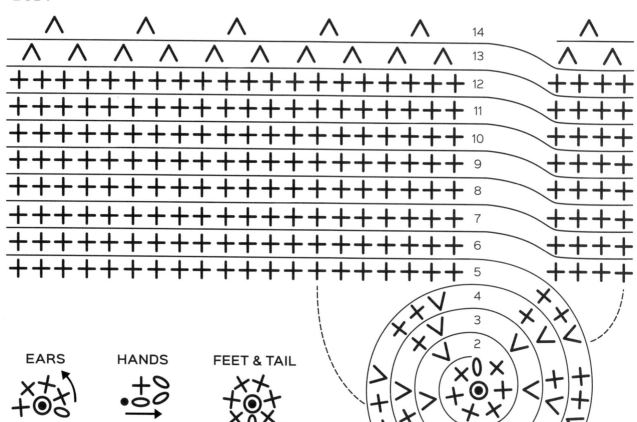

EARS

HANDS

FEET & TAIL

KEY

- • start
- O adjustable ring
- ⊂ chain
- ⬬ slip stitch
- ✛ double crochet
- T half treble crochet
- Ŧ treble crochet
- V 2 double crochet in 1 stitch
- Λ double crochet 2 together

Body

The bear's body is crocheted from top to bottom. Work in the round, without joining rounds. Using body colour, start with an adjustable ring.
1 6 dc into ring.
2 2 dc in each st around (12 dc).
3 (2 dc in next st, dc in next st) 6 times (18 dc).
4 (2 dc in next st, dc in next 2 sts) 6 times (24 dc).
5–7 Dc in each st around, for 3 rounds (24 dc per round).
Change to pyjama colour.
8–12 Dc in each st around, for 5 rounds (24 dc per round).
13 (Dc2tog) 12 times (12 sts). Stuff the body, making it nice and puffy.
14 (Dc2tog) 6 times (6 sts). Cut yarn, leaving a long tail for sewing, and finish off. Add a little more stuffing if necessary, then sew the hole closed.

Ears

(make 2)
Using body colour, start with an adjustable ring.
1 4 dc into ring.
Do not join round. Cut yarn, leaving a long tail for sewing, and finish off.

Hands

(make 2)
Using body colour, ch 3.
1 Dc in the very first ch. Cut yarn, leaving a long tail for sewing, and finish off.

Feet and tail

(make 3)
Using body colour, start with an adjustable ring.
1 6 dc into ring.
Cut yarn, leaving a long tail for sewing, and finish off. Join round.

Finishing

Use black yarn to embroider two eyes onto your bear's head, between rounds 6 and 7 of the body and about 4 stitches apart.

To make the felt snout, first cut a ⅜ in (1cm) square out of off-white craft felt. Cut away the corners of the square to make a round snout shape. Use matching thread to sew the snout onto your bear's face, in line with rounds 6 and 7 of the body.
With black thread, sew a small mouth and nose onto the snout.
Sew the ears on top of the head, in line with rounds 3 and 4 of the body.
Sew the hands in place, in line with round 9 of the body and about 5 stitches apart.
Sew the feet onto your bear, in line with rounds 12 and 13 of the body.
Finally, sew the tail onto the back of your bear, in line with the feet.

Actual size

Size

Using the suggested yarn and hook, your fox's body will be about 2in (5cm) long.

You will need

Medium-weight yarn in body colour – approx 22yd (20m)
Medium-weight yarn in black – approx 5½yd (5m)
Medium-weight yarn in white – approx 2yd (2m)
Crochet hook – 3.5mm (UK9:USE/4)
Toy stuffing
Yarn needle
Craft felt in white
Embroidery needle
Embroidery thread in white and black

Abbreviations

See page 154

Fox

This fox has a long, white-tipped tail and
a slightly pointy nose. Its face is made
by sewing a white felt beard onto the head,
and embroidering some eyes and a nose.
The amigurumi fox's black crocheted paws
and ears stand out nicely against an orange
or reddish-brown body.

BODY

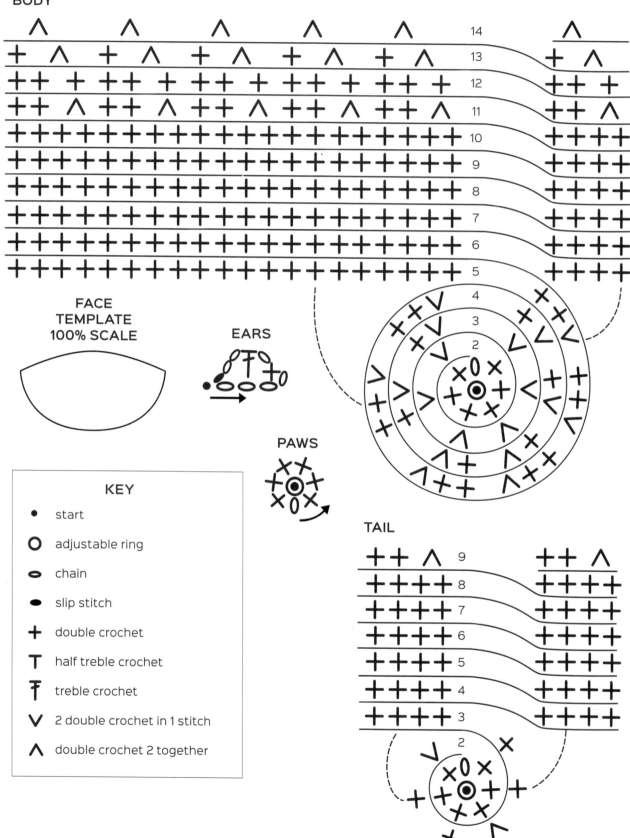

FACE
TEMPLATE
100% SCALE

EARS

PAWS

TAIL

KEY

- • start
- O adjustable ring
- ⬭ chain
- ⬬ slip stitch
- + double crochet
- T half treble crochet
- Ŧ treble crochet
- V 2 double crochet in 1 stitch
- ∧ double crochet 2 together

Body

The fox's body is crocheted from back to front. Work in the round, without joining rounds.

Using body colour, start with an adjustable ring.

1 6 dc into ring.

2 2 dc in each st around (12 dc).

3 (2 dc in next st, dc in next st) 6 times (18 dc).

4 (2 dc in next st, dc in next 2 sts) 6 times (24 dc).

5–10 Dc in each st around, for 6 rounds (24 dc per round).

11 (Dc2tog, dc in next 2 sts) 6 times (18 sts).

12 Dc in each st around (18 dc).

13 (Dc2tog, dc in next st) 6 times (12 sts).

Stuff the body, making it nice and puffy.

14 (Dc2tog) 6 times (6 sts).

Cut yarn, leaving a long tail for sewing, and finish off. Add a little more stuffing if necessary, then sew the hole closed.

Tail

Using white yarn, start with an adjustable ring.

1 6 dc into ring.

2 (2 dc in next st, dc in next 2 sts) twice (8 dc).

Change to body colour yarn.

3–8 Dc in each st around, for 6 rounds (8 dc per round).

9 (Dc2tog, dc in next 2 sts) twice (6 sts).

Cut yarn, leaving a long tail for sewing, and finish off.

Paws

(make 4)

Using black yarn, start with an adjustable ring.

1 6 dc into ring.

Cut yarn, leaving a long tail for sewing, and finish off. Join round.

Ears

(make 2)

Using black yarn, ch 4.

1 (Dc, ch 1) in 2nd ch from hook, (tr, ch 2) in next ch, sl st in last ch.

Cut yarn, leaving a long tail for sewing, and finish off.

Finishing

Sew the tail onto the back of your fox's body, right in the middle.

Sew the four paws onto the bottom of your fox. The back paws should line up with rounds 5 and 6 of the body; the front paws should line up with rounds 9 and 10. You can pin them in place to make sure they are straight before sewing.

Trace the face shape onto white felt, and cut it out. Use white thread to sew the felt in place, covering the bottom half of your fox's face.

Use black yarn to embroider two eyes onto the face, just above the white felt beard. With black thread, sew a small nose and mouth onto the white felt.

Sew the ears on top of the head, in line with round 10 of the body and about 4 stitches apart.

Actual size

Size
Using the suggested yarn and hook, your owl's body will be about 2in (5cm) tall.

You will need
Medium-weight yarn in main colour – approx 22yd (20m)
Crochet hook – 3.5mm (UK9:USE/4)
Toy stuffing
Yarn needle
Craft felt in off-white and brown
Embroidery needle
Embroidery thread in off-white and brown

Abbreviations
See page 154

Owl

The amigurumi owl has a pudgy body, crocheted
wings, and two tiny ears on top. A heart-shaped
felt face is sewn onto the head, with a small
embroidered beak. Felt is used for the eyes to
make them extra large and round – all the
better to see you with.

BODY

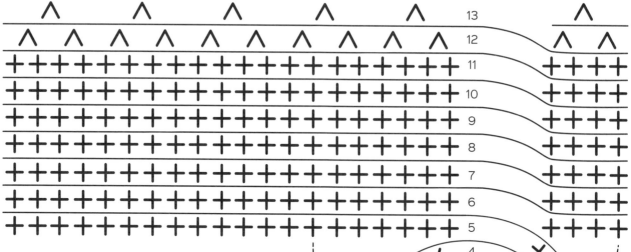

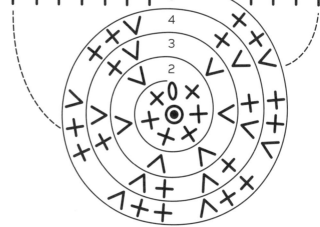

KEY

- **•** start
- **O** adjustable ring
- **⊖** chain
- **⬬** slip stitch
- **+** double crochet
- **T** half treble crochet
- **T̄** treble crochet
- **V** 2 double crochet in 1 stitch
- **∧** double crochet 2 together

WINGS

TAIL

EARS

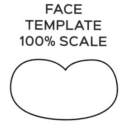

FACE TEMPLATE 100% SCALE

Body

The owl's body is crocheted from top to bottom. Work in the round, without joining rounds.

Using main colour, start with an adjustable ring.

1 6 dc into ring.

2 2 dc in each st around (12 dc).

3 (2 dc in next st, dc in next st) 6 times (18 dc).

4 (2 dc in next st, dc in next 2 sts) 6 times (24 dc).

5–11 Dc in each st around, for 7 rounds (24 dc per round).

12 (Dc2tog) 12 times (12 sts). Stuff the body, making it nice and puffy.

13 (Dc2tog) 6 times (6 sts). Cut yarn, leaving a long tail for sewing, and finish off. Add a little more stuffing if necessary, then sew the hole closed.

Wings

(make 2)

Using main colour, start with an adjustable ring.

1 (Dc, htr, 2 tr, htr, dc) into ring (6 sts).

Do not join the round. Cut the yarn, leaving a long tail for sewing, and finish off.

Tail

Using main colour, start with an adjustable ring.

1 4 dc into ring.

Do not join the round. Cut the yarn, leaving a long tail for sewing, and finish off.

Ears

(make 2)

Using main colour, ch 3.

1 Dc in very first ch.

Cut yarn, leaving a long tail for sewing, and finish off.

Finishing

Use the template to cut a face shape out of off-white craft felt. With matching thread, sew the face onto the front of your owl, in line with rounds 5 to 7 of the body.

To make the eyes, cut two ⅜in (1cm) squares out of brown felt. Cut away the corners of the squares to make two small circles. Use brown thread to sew the eye circles onto the felt face.

With brown thread, embroider a tiny beak in between the eyes.

Sew the wings onto the sides of your owl, between rounds 7 and 8 of the body and about 8 stitches apart.

Sew the tail onto the back of your owl, between rounds 10 and 11 of the body.

Sew the ears on top of the head, in line with round 3 of the body.

Actual size

Size
Using the suggested yarn and hook, your raccoon's body will be about 2in (5cm) tall.

You will need
Medium-weight yarn in grey – approx 22yd (20m)
Medium-weight yarn in black – approx 11yd (10m)
Crochet hook – 3.5mm (UK9:USE/4)
Toy stuffing
Yarn needle
Craft felt in white and dark brown
Embroidery needle
Embroidery thread in white, dark brown and black

Abbreviations
See page 154

Raccoon

This raccoon has a simple grey body and a long striped tail. The face is made with felt shapes and embroidered details. Tiny crocheted ears, hands and feet are sewn on next. With its roly-poly shape, the amigurumi raccoon is not quite as nimble as its real-life counterpart.

BODY

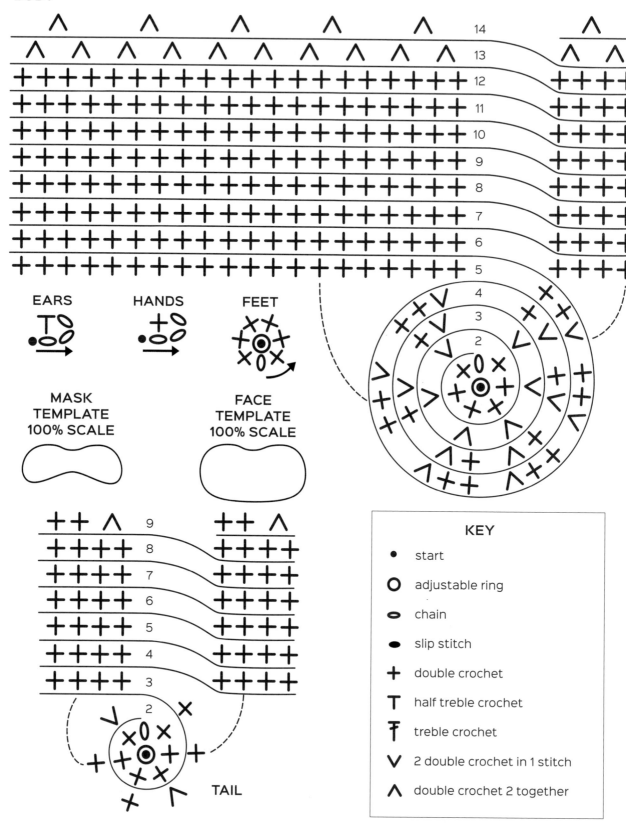

EARS

HANDS

FEET

MASK
TEMPLATE
100% SCALE

FACE
TEMPLATE
100% SCALE

TAIL

KEY

- • start
- O adjustable ring
- ⊖ chain
- ⬤ slip stitch
- + double crochet
- T half treble crochet
- Ŧ treble crochet
- V 2 double crochet in 1 stitch
- ∧ double crochet 2 together

Body

The raccoon's body is crocheted from top to bottom. Work in the round, without joining rounds. Using grey yarn, start with an adjustable ring.
1 6 dc into ring.
2 2 dc in each st around (12 dc).
3 (2 dc in next st, dc in next st) 6 times (18 dc).
4 (2 dc in next st, dc in next 2 sts) 6 times (24 dc).
5–12 Dc in each st around, for 8 rounds (24 dc per round).
13 (Dc2tog) 12 times (12 sts). Stuff the body, making it nice and puffy.
14 (Dc2tog) 6 times (6 sts). Cut yarn, leaving a long tail for sewing, and finish off. Add a little more stuffing if necessary, then sew the hole closed.

Ears

(make 2)
Using black yarn, ch 3.
1 Htr in the very first ch. Cut yarn, leaving a long tail for sewing, and finish off.

Hands

(make 2)
Using black yarn, ch 3.
1 Dc in the very first ch. Cut yarn, leaving a long tail for sewing, and finish off.

Feet

(make 2)
Using black yarn, start with an adjustable ring.
1 6 dc into ring. Cut yarn, leaving a long tail for sewing, and finish off. Join round.

Tail

Using black yarn, start with an adjustable ring.
1 6 dc into ring.
2 (2 dc in next st, dc in next 2 sts) twice (8 dc). Change to grey yarn.
3–8 Dc in each st around, for 6 rounds (8 dc per round).
9 (Dc2tog, dc in next 2 sts) twice (6 sts). Cut yarn, leaving a long tail for sewing, and finish off. To make the tail stripes, take a length of black yarn and wind it around the tail 3 times. Secure the ends of the black yarn inside the tail.

Finishing

Use the templates to cut one face shape out of white felt, and one mask shape out of brown felt.

With white thread, sew the face shape in place, in line with rounds 4 to 7 of the body. Use brown thread to sew the brown felt mask onto the white face.
With black thread, sew two eyes onto the mask. Embroider a small mouth and nose onto the white face, just below the mask.
Sew the ears on top of your raccoon's head, in line with rounds 3 and 4 of the body. The half treble stitch of the ear should lie against the head.
Sew the hands just below the face, in line with round 9 of the body and about 4 stitches apart.
Attach the feet onto the front of your raccoon, in line with rounds 11 and 12 of the body.
Sew the tail onto the back in line with round 12 of the body, making sure your raccoon can sit up straight.

Actual size

Size

Using the suggested yarn and hook, your squirrel's body will be about 2in (5cm) tall.

You will need

Medium-weight yarn in brown – approx 33yd (30m)
Medium-weight yarn in black – approx 1yd (1m)
Crochet hook – 3.5mm (UK9:USE/4)
Yarn needle
Toy stuffing
Craft felt in off-white
Embroidery needle
Embroidery thread in off-white and black

Abbreviations

See page 154

Squirrel

Amigurumi squirrels have nice bushy tails, which can be made even bushier by brushing the yarn with a stiff brush. A cute felt tummy is sewn onto the round body, along with a face, ears, hands and feet. Squirrels can come in many different shades of brown.

BODY

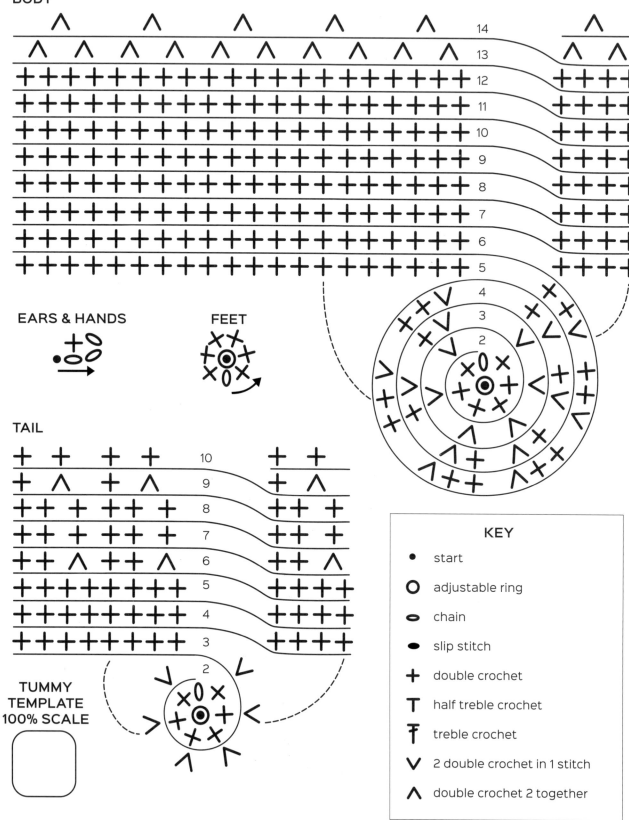

EARS & HANDS

FEET

TAIL

TUMMY TEMPLATE
100% SCALE

KEY

- **•** start
- **O** adjustable ring
- **⊂** chain
- **⊂** slip stitch
- **+** double crochet
- **T** half treble crochet
- **Ŧ** treble crochet
- **V** 2 double crochet in 1 stitch
- **Λ** double crochet 2 together

Body

The squirrel's body is crocheted from top to bottom. Work in the round, without joining rounds. Using brown yarn, start with an adjustable ring

1 6 dc into ring.

2 2 dc in each st around (12 dc).

3 (2 dc in next st, dc in next st) 6 times (18 dc).

4 (2 dc in next st, dc in next 2 sts) 6 times (24 dc).

5–12 Dc in each st around, for 8 rounds (24 dc per round).

13 (Dc2tog) 12 times (12 sts). Stuff the body, making it nice and puffy.

14 (Dc2tog) 6 times (6 sts). Cut yarn, leaving a long tail for sewing, and finish off. Add a little more stuffing if necessary, then sew the hole closed.

Ears and hands

(make 4)
Using brown yarn, ch 3.

1 Dc in the very first ch. Cut yarn, leaving a long tail for sewing, and finish off.

Feet

(make 2)
Using brown yarn, start with an adjustable ring.

1 6 dc into ring. Cut yarn, leaving a long tail for sewing, and finish off. Join round.

Tail

Using black yarn, start with an adjustable ring.

1 6 dc into ring.

2 2 dc in each st around (12 dc).

3–5 Dc in each st around, for 3 rounds (12 dc per round).

6 (Dc2tog, dc in next 2 sts) 3 times (9 sts). Stuff the tail lightly.

7–8 Dc in each st around, for 2 rounds (9 dc per round).

9 (Dc2tog, dc in next st) 3 times (6 sts).

10 Dc in each st around (6 dc). Cut yarn, leaving a long tail for sewing, and finish off.

Finishing

Use black yarn to sew two eyes onto your squirrel's face, between rounds 6 and 7 of the body and about 4 stitches apart.

With black thread, embroider a mouth and nose by sewing a small T-shape in between the eyes.

Use the template to cut a tummy shape out of off-white craft felt. Using off-white thread, sew the tummy onto the front of your squirrel, in line with rounds 8 to 11 of the body.

Sew the ears on top of the head, in line with round 3 of the body.

Attach the hands on either side of the tummy, in line with round 8 of the body.

Sew the feet on either side of the tummy, in line with rounds 11 and 12 of the body. If you are making an extra-fluffy tail, use a stiff wire brush to brush out the tail piece.

Sew the tail onto the back of your squirrel, in line with round 12 of the body. Use a few extra stitches to hold the tail up against the squirrel's back.

Zoo Animals

Actual size

Size

Using the suggested yarn and hook, your elephant's body will be about 2½in (6cm) long.

You will need

Medium-weight yarn in grey – approx 33yd (30m)
Medium-weight yarn in black – approx 1yd (1m)
Crochet hook – 3.5mm (UK9:USE/4)
Yarn needle
Toy stuffing
Craft felt in pink
Embroidery needle
Embroidery thread in pink

Abbreviations

See page 154

Elephant

The elephant is the largest of all the mini amigurumi animals. Its body and trunk are crocheted all in one piece, from back to front. The face, feet, ears and tail are sewn on next. Felt is added inside the ears for a little pop of colour on an otherwise grey amigurumi.

BODY

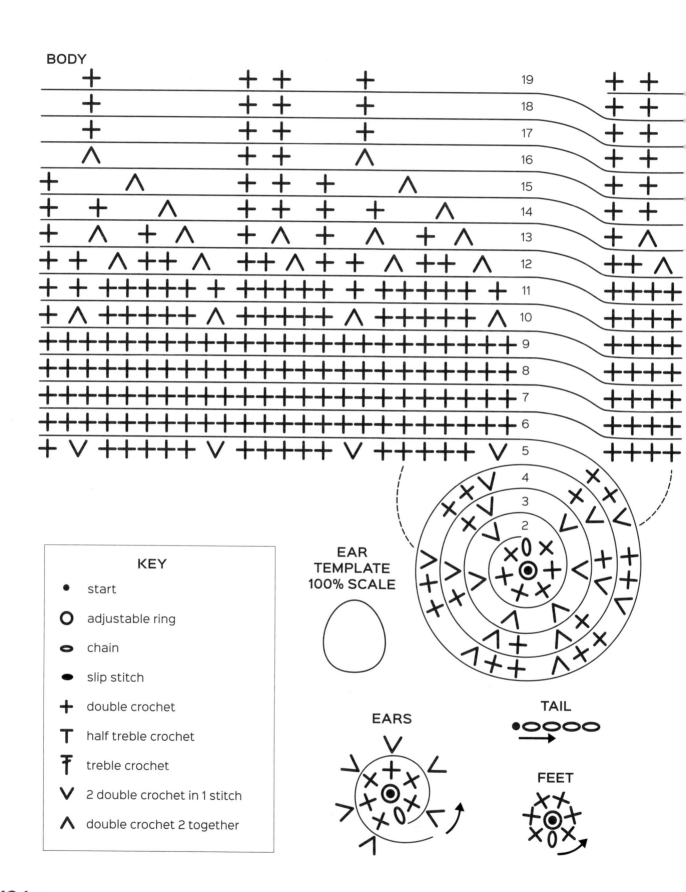

KEY

- • start
- O adjustable ring
- ⊖ chain
- ⬬ slip stitch
- + double crochet
- T half treble crochet
- 𝕋 treble crochet
- V 2 double crochet in 1 stitch
- ∧ double crochet 2 together

EAR
TEMPLATE
100% SCALE

EARS

TAIL

FEET

Body

The elephant's body is crocheted from back to front. Work in the round, without joining rounds. Using grey yarn, start with an adjustable ring.

1 6 dc into ring.

2 2 dc in each st around (12 dc).

3 (2 dc in next st, dc in next st) 6 times (18 dc).

4 (2 dc in next st, dc in next 2 sts) 6 times (24 dc).

5 (2 dc in next st, dc in next 5 sts) 4 times (28 dc).

6–9 Dc in each st around, for 4 rounds (28 dc per round).

10 (Dc2tog, dc in next 5 sts) 4 times (24 sts).

11 Dc in each st around (24 dc).

12 (Dc2tog, dc in next 2 sts) 6 times (18 sts).

13 (Dc2tog, dc in next st) 6 times (12 sts).

14 (Dc2tog, dc in next 4 sts) twice (10 sts).

Stuff the body, making it nice and puffy.

15 (Dc2tog, dc in next 3 sts) twice (8 sts).

16 (Dc2tog, dc in next 2 sts) twice (6 sts).

17–19 Dc in each st around, for 3 rounds (6 dc per round).

Cut yarn, leaving a long tail for sewing, and finish off. Sew the hole closed, then use the remaining tail to sew the tip of the trunk down, between rounds 12 and 13 of the elephant's body.

Feet

(make 2)

Using grey yarn, start with an adjustable ring.

1 6 dc into ring.

Cut yarn, leaving a long tail for sewing, and finish off. Join round.

Ears

(make 2)

Using grey yarn, start with an adjustable ring.

1 6 dc into ring.

2 2 dc in each st around (12 dc).

Do not join round. Cut yarn, leaving a long tail for sewing, and finish off.

Tail

Using grey yarn, ch 4. Cut yarn, leaving a long tail for sewing, and finish off.

Finishing

Use black yarn to embroider some eyes on either side of the trunk, in line with round 12 of the elephant's body. Sew the feet evenly onto the bottom of your elephant. The back feet should line up with rounds 5 and 6 of the body; the front feet should line up with rounds 9 and 10.

You can pin the feet in place to make sure your elephant stands up straight before sewing them on. Use the template to cut two ear shapes out of pink felt. Using pink thread, sew the felt ear shapes onto the inside of the crocheted ears. Sew the ears onto either side of the head, between rounds 9 and 10 of the body. For the tail, sew one end of the chain onto the back of your elephant, between rounds 3 and 4 of the body. Trim the yarn tail on the other end, leaving a little tuft of yarn.

Actual size

Size

Using the suggested yarn and hook, your hippo's body will be about 2in (5cm) long.

You will need

Medium-weight yarn in main colour – approx 27yd (25m)
Medium-weight yarn in black – approx 1yd (1m)
Crochet hook – 3.5mm (UK9:USE/4)
Toy stuffing
Yarn needle
Embroidery needle
Embroidery thread in black

Abbreviations

See page 154

Hippo

This amigurumi hippo has a nice plump body
and an oval snout. It is crocheted all in
one colour, displaying a simple embroidered
face. Despite its short legs and rotund body,
this hippo is in fact faster and more buoyant
than you might think. Make lots of amigurumi
friends to keep your hippo happy.

BODY

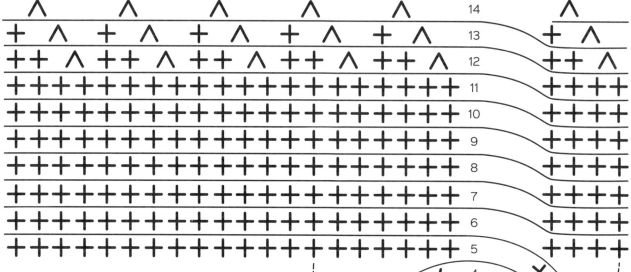

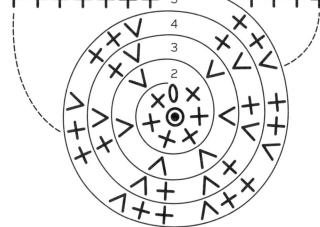

KEY

- •   start
- O   adjustable ring
- ⊘   chain
- ⬮   slip stitch
- **+**   double crochet
- **T**   half treble crochet
- **Ŧ**   treble crochet
- **V**   2 double crochet in 1 stitch
- **Λ**   double crochet 2 together

EARS

MUZZLE

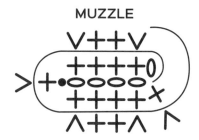

FEET

Body

The hippo's body is crocheted from back to front. Work in the round, without joining rounds. Using main colour, start with an adjustable ring.
1 6 dc into ring.
2 2 dc in each st around (12 dc).
3 (2 dc in next st, dc in next st) 6 times (18 dc).
4 (2 dc in next st, dc in next 2 sts) 6 times (24 dc).
5–11 Dc in each st around, for 7 rounds (24 dc per round).
12 (Dc2tog, dc in next 2 sts) 6 times (18 sts).
13 (Dc2tog, dc in next st) 6 times (12 sts).
Stuff the body, making it nice and puffy.
14 (Dc2tog) 6 times (6 sts).
Cut yarn, leaving a long tail for sewing, and finish off. Add a little more stuffing if necessary, then sew the hole closed.

Feet

(make 4)
Using main colour, start with an adjustable ring.
1 6 dc into ring.
Cut yarn, leaving a long tail for sewing, and finish off. Join round.

Muzzle

Using main colour, ch 5.
1 Dc in 2nd ch from hook, dc in next 2 ch, 3 dc in last ch. Rotate your work so that you can crochet back down the bottom of the starting chain. Dc in next 2 ch, 2 dc in last ch (10 dc).
2 2 dc in first stitch of round 1, dc in next 2 sts, 2 dc in each of next 3 sts, dc in next 2 sts, 2 dc in each of next 2 sts (16 dc).
Cut yarn, leaving a long tail for sewing, and finish off. Join round.

Ears

(make 2)
Using main colour, start with an adjustable ring.
1 3 dc into ring.
Do not join round. Cut yarn, leaving a long tail for sewing, and finish off.

Finishing

Sew the four feet onto the bottom of your hippo. The back feet should line up with rounds 5 and 6 of the body, and the front feet should line up with rounds 9 and 10. You can pin the feet in place to make sure they are straight.
Sew the muzzle onto the front of your hippo.
Sew the ears in place, between rounds 11 and 12 of the body and about 8 stitches apart.
Use black yarn to sew the eyes on either side of the muzzle.
With black thread, embroider two little nostrils and a tiny mouth onto the muzzle.

Actual size

Size

Using the suggested yarn and hook, your lion's body will be about 2in (5cm) long.

You will need

Medium-weight yarn in body colour – approx 22yd (20m)
Medium-weight yarn in mane colour – approx 5½yd (5m)
Medium-weight yarn in black – approx 1yd (1m)
Crochet hook – 3.5mm (UK9:USE/4)
Toy stuffing
Yarn needle
Craft felt in off-white
Embroidery needle
Embroidery thread in black and off-white

Abbreviations

See page 154

Lion

Here is a grand little lion, with a nice
crocheted mane and an embroidered felt snout.
The paws, tail and other details are all sewn
onto a good rounded body. This amigurumi lion
likes to spend time with family, and can be
just as friendly as its amigurumi cat cousin.

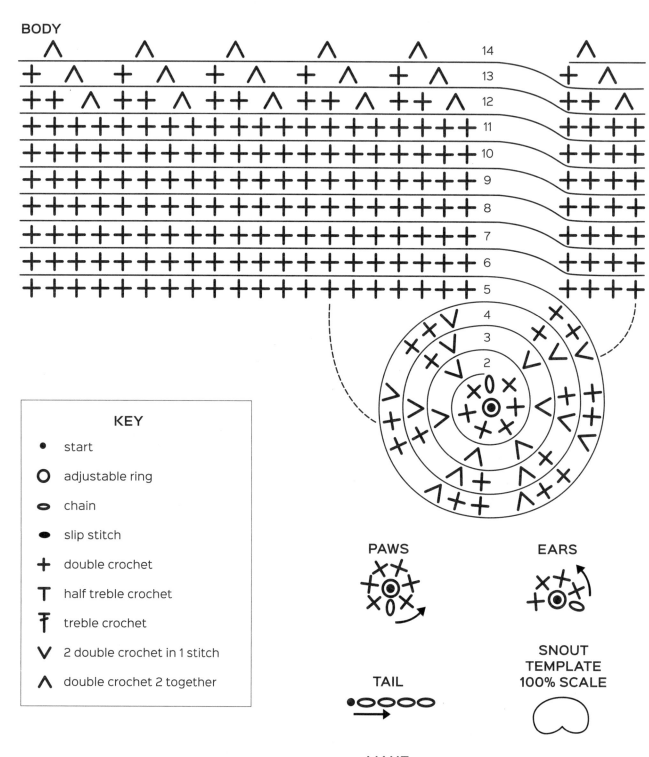

BODY

KEY

- **•** start
- **O** adjustable ring
- **⬬** chain
- **⬬** slip stitch
- **+** double crochet
- **T** half treble crochet
- **Ŧ** treble crochet
- **V** 2 double crochet in 1 stitch
- **Λ** double crochet 2 together

PAWS

EARS

SNOUT TEMPLATE 100% SCALE

TAIL

MANE

Body

The lion's body is crocheted from back to front. Work in the round, without joining rounds.

Using body colour yarn, start with an adjustable ring.

1 6 dc into ring.

2 2 dc in each st around (12 dc).

3 (2 dc in next st, dc in next st) 6 times (18 dc).

4 (2 dc in next st, dc in next 2 sts) 6 times (24 dc).

5–11 Dc in each st around, for 7 rounds (24 dc per round).

12 (Dc2tog, dc in next 2 sts) 6 times (18 sts).

13 (Dc2tog, dc in next st) 6 times (12 sts).

Stuff the body, making it nice and puffy.

14 (Dc2tog) 6 times (6 sts).

Cut yarn, leaving a long tail for sewing, and finish off. Add a little more stuffing if necessary, then sew the hole closed.

Paws

(make 4)

Using body colour yarn, start with an adjustable ring.

1 6 dc into ring.

Cut yarn, leaving a long tail for sewing, and finish off. Join round.

Mane

Using mane colour yarn, ch 22.

1 Sl st in 2nd ch from hook, 4 dc in next ch, sl st in next ch (sl st in next ch, 4 htr in next ch, sl st in next ch) 5 times. Sl st in next ch, 4 dc in next ch, sl st in next ch.

Cut yarn, leaving a long tail for sewing, and finish off.

Ears

(make 2)

Using body colour yarn, start with an adjustable ring.

1 4 dc into ring.

Do not join round. Cut yarn, leaving a long tail for sewing, and finish off.

Tail

Using body colour yarn, ch 4.

Cut yarn, leaving a long tail for sewing, and finish off.

Finishing

Sew the paws onto the bottom of your lion. The back paws should line up with rounds 5 and 6 of the body; the front paws should line up with rounds 9 and 10. You can pin them in place to make sure they are straight before sewing. Use black yarn to embroider the eyes onto the face, in line with round 12 of the body.

Cut one snout shape out of off-white craft felt. Use matching thread to sew the snout onto the lion's face, in between the eyes.

With black thread, sew a T-shape onto the felt snout to make the nose.

Sew the mane around your lion's head, between rounds 9 and 10 of the body.

Sew the ears on top of the head, between rounds 10 and 11 of the body and about 4 stitches apart.

Add the tail by sewing one end of the chain onto the back of your lion, between rounds 3 and 4 of the body. Trim the yarn tail on the other end, leaving a little tuft of yarn.

Actual size

Size

Using the suggested yarn and hook, your panda's body will be about 2in (5cm) tall.

You will need

Medium-weight yarn in white – approx 16 ½yd (15m)
Medium-weight yarn in black – approx 16 ½yd (15m)
Crochet hook – 3.5mm (UK9:USE/4)
Toy stuffing
Yarn needle
Craft felt in black
Embroidery needle
Embroidery thread in black

Abbreviations

See page 154

Panda

Amigurumi pandas are usually quiet, docile
creatures. Their bodies are crocheted from top
to bottom, with a black stripe in the middle.
The felt eye patches and face are sewn onto
the body, along with some arms, legs and ears.
Be sure to keep your mini panda well fed.

BODY

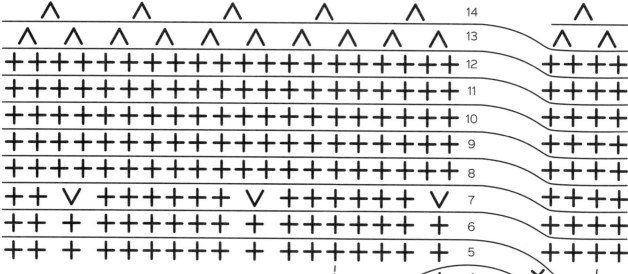

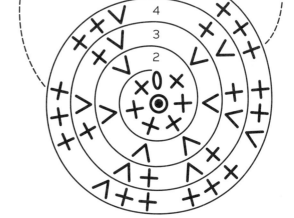

KEY

- •   start
- O   adjustable ring
- ⬭   chain
- ⬬   slip stitch
- ✚   double crochet
- T   half treble crochet
- Ŧ   treble crochet
- V   2 double crochet in 1 stitch
- ∧   double crochet 2 together

ARMS & LEGS

TAIL

EARS

EYE PATCH TEMPLATES 100% SCALE

Body

The panda's body is crocheted from top to bottom. Work in the round, without joining rounds. Using white yarn, start with an adjustable ring.

1 6 dc into ring.

2 2 dc in each st around (12 dc).

3 (2 dc in next st, dc in next st) 6 times (18 dc).

4 (2 dc in next st, dc in next 5 sts) 3 times (21 dc).

5–6 Dc in each st around, for 2 rounds (21 dc per round).

7 (2 dc in next st, dc in next 6 sts) 3 times (24 dc). Change to black yarn.

8–9 Dc in each st around, for 2 rounds (24 dc per round). Change to white yarn.

10–12 Dc in each st around, for 3 rounds (24 dc per round).

13 (Dc2tog) 12 times (12 sts). Stuff the body, making it nice and puffy.

14 (Dc2tog) 6 times (6 sts). Cut yarn, leaving a long tail for sewing, and finish off. Add a little more stuffing if necessary, then sew the hole closed.

Arms and legs

(make 4)

Using black yarn, ch 7.

1 Htr in 2nd ch from hook, htr in next 5 ch (6 htr). Cut yarn, leaving a long tail for sewing, and finish off.

Tail

Using white yarn, start with an adjustable ring.

1 6 dc into ring. Cut yarn, leaving a long tail for sewing, and finish off. Join round.

Ears

(make 2)

Using black yarn, start with an adjustable ring.

1 3 dc into ring. Do not join round. Cut yarn, leaving a long tail for sewing, and finish off.

Finishing

Use the template to cut two eye patches out of black craft felt. Sew the eye patches onto your panda's face, in line with rounds 5 to 7 of the body.

With black thread, embroider an eye in the middle of each felt eye patch. Use a few small stitches to make a nose and mouth.

Sew the two arms in place, in line with the black stripe on the body.

Sew the two legs in line with round 12 of the body.

Sew the tail onto the back of your panda, in line with the legs.

Sew the ears on top of the head, in line with rounds 3 and 4 of the body.

Actual size

Size

Using the suggested yarn and hook, your sloth's body will be about 2in (5cm) tall.

You will need

Medium-weight yarn in brown – approx 22yd (20m)
Crochet hook – 3.5mm (UK9:USE/4)
Toy stuffing
Yarn needle
Craft felt in off-white and dark brown
Embroidery needle
Embroidery thread in off-white, dark brown and black

Abbreviations

See page 154

Sloth

An amigurumi sloth has a plump body and
long crocheted limbs. The position of the arms
and legs can be changed to give it different
poses. A sloth face is made by sewing felt
shapes onto the body, with an embroidered nose
and mouth. This sloth is one of the calmest
amigurumi creatures.

BODY

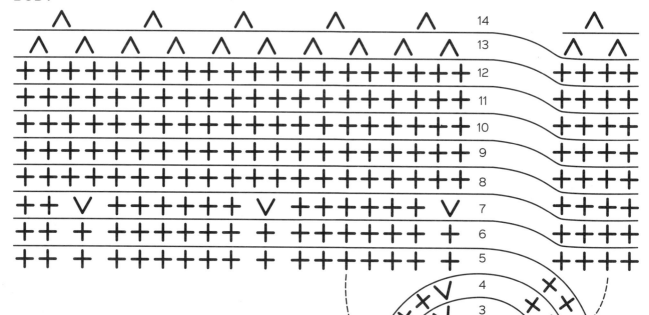

KEY

- ● start
- O adjustable ring
- ◔ chain
- ◖ slip stitch
- ✚ double crochet
- T half treble crochet
- Ŧ treble crochet
- V 2 double crochet in 1 stitch
- ∧ double crochet 2 together

ARMS & LEGS

FACE TEMPLATE 100% SCALE

EYE TEMPLATES 100% SCALE

Body

The sloth's body is crocheted from top to bottom. Work in the round, without joining rounds. Using brown yarn, start with an adjustable ring.

1 6 dc into ring.

2 2 dc in each st around (12 dc).

3 (2 dc in next st, dc in next st) 6 times (18 dc).

4 (2 dc in next st, dc in next 5 sts) 3 times (21 dc).

5–6 Dc in each st around, for 2 rounds (21 dc per round).

7 (2 dc in next st, dc in next 6 sts) 3 times (24 dc).

8–12 Dc in each st around, for 5 rounds (24 dc per round).

13 (Dc2tog) 12 times (12 sts). Stuff the body, making it nice and puffy.

14 (Dc2tog) 6 times (6 sts). Cut yarn, leaving a long tail for sewing, and finish off. Add a little more stuffing if necessary, then sew the hole closed.

Arms and legs

(make 4)

Using brown yarn, ch 7.

1 Htr in 2nd ch from hook, htr in next 5 ch (6 htr). Cut yarn, leaving a long tail for sewing, and finish off.

Finishing

Using the templates, cut one off-white face and two dark brown eye shapes out of felt.

With off-white thread, sew the face shape onto your sloth's head, in line with rounds 4 to 7 of the body. Use dark brown thread to sew the eye shapes onto the face.

With black thread, embroider a mouth and nose, using small, straight sts. Embroider some eyes onto the felt eye shapes. Sew the two arms in place, in line with rounds 8 and 9 of the body. Sew the two legs in line with rounds 11 and 12 of the body.

Tools and materials

At the beginning of each project, you will find a list of the materials and tools used to make your amigurumi creature. Here we explain in a little more detail the items you will need.

1 Yarn

Since exact size is not important for amigurumi, there is a lot of room to play with different types of yarn. The patterns in this book are written for medium-weight yarn (also called worsted, Afghan or Aran yarn). However, most of the patterns will work just as well with thicker or thinner yarn.

You can experiment with different fibre contents, too. Acrylic yarn is readily available, comes in a large variety of colours, and is easy to work with. Wool has a nice warm feel, and is great for making fuzzy animals. Cotton has good stitch definition, but can sometimes be quite stiff, making it difficult to crochet small items. It is best to choose yarn that feels nice to the touch, so that you will enjoy working with it.

2 Crochet hook

Choose a crochet hook that is a few sizes smaller than that recommended on the yarn label. If your hook is too large, there will be holes in the crocheted fabric, and the stuffing will show through. For these patterns, a 3.5mm (UK9/ USE/4) hook is used with medium-weight yarn. If you find your hands get sore or your crocheted pieces feel very stiff, try a slightly larger hook.

3 Stuffing

Polyester toy stuffing is recommended, and can be found in most craft stores. Since each amigurumi only requires a small amount, a small bag of stuffing goes a long way. If no toy stuffing is available, you could use the insides of an old cushion or pillow instead.

4 Craft felt

Add small shapes to your amigurumi using craft felt. Choose the thinnest type of felt available, which is usually ¹⁄₃₂in (1mm) thick. You will only need a tiny bit of felt for each animal.

5 Embroidery thread

Sew small details onto your amigurumi with embroidery thread. Any kind of coloured thread can be used, but good-quality embroidery thread will look best.

6 Embroidery needle

An embroidery needle is used when sewing with thread. You can substitute any hand-sewing needle, as long as it is small and has a sharp tip.

7 Yarn needle

A yarn needle is used to sew crocheted pieces together. It has a blunt tip, and an eye that is big enough to thread your yarn through. It is also called a tapestry needle or darning needle.

8 Pins

Use pins to hold parts of your amigurumi in place before sewing them together. Choose the kind with a large round head, so that they don't get lost inside.

9 Stitch markers

Stitch markers can be used to mark the beginning of a round, making it easier to count the stitches. A paperclip or safety pin can be used as a makeshift stitch marker.

10 Wire brush

To make an extra-fluffy amigurumi, use a wire brush to brush out the yarn. Choose one with very stiff bristles, such as a wire pet grooming brush. This technique works well with wool and most acrylic yarn, but may not work with cotton or micro-spun acrylic.

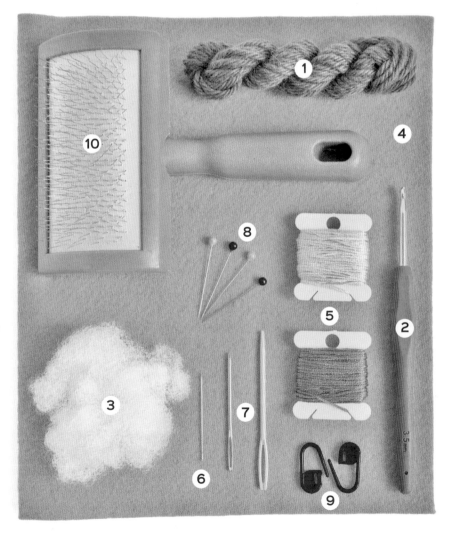

Techniques

This section outlines all the techniques you will need to make the mini crochet creatures in this book.

Holding the hook

Hold the crochet hook in your dominant hand. Place your thumb on the thumb rest (the flattened area in the middle of the crochet hook) and support the handle with your last three fingers. If necessary, you can use your forefinger to help guide the yarn while crocheting.

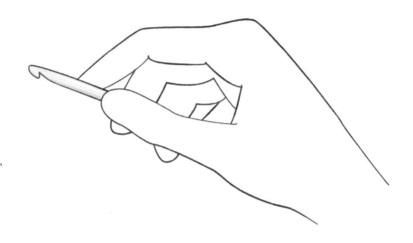

Holding the yarn

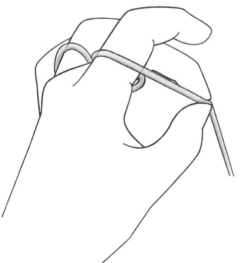

Hold the yarn in your non-dominant hand. Wrap the ball end of the yarn over the back of your forefinger, and hold the working yarn between your thumb and middle finger. Use your forefinger to regulate the tension as you crochet. You can wrap the ball end over your ring finger to help with tension.

Holding your hook and yarn in the correct way will make it easier to crochet even stitches, resulting in a neater-looking amigurumi. Comfort is the most important thing: be sure not to grip too tightly, and try different positions if your hands feel uncomfortable.

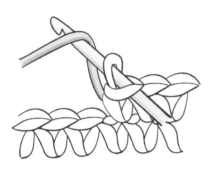

Yarn over

Wrap the working yarn over the top of your crochet hook, from back to front.

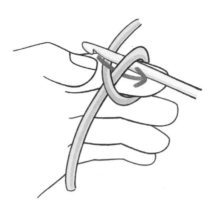

Adjustable ring

Form a loop around your index finger by wrapping the ball end of the yarn over the tail end. Slide your hook underneath the loop, grab the working end of the yarn, and pull it through. Slide the ring off your finger. Yarn over and

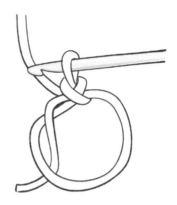

pull the yarn through the loop on your hook. You are now ready to make the first round of stitches. After working the first round into the ring, pull on the tail end to close the hole in the middle.

Slip knot

Place the tail end of the yarn over the ball end, forming a loop. Insert your hook into the loop, grab the tail end and pull it through. Pull on the ends to tighten the knot, leaving a loop on your crochet hook.

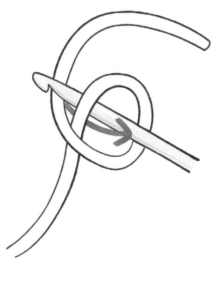

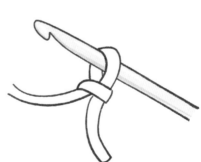

Foundation chain

Start with a slip knot. Yarn over and pull the yarn through the loop on your hook. This counts as one chain. Repeat to create as many chains as required.

The front of the chain should look like a row of V-shapes, while the back has a row of ridges. To work a stitch into the foundation chain, insert your hook underneath the top loop and the back ridge loop, then make the desired stitch.

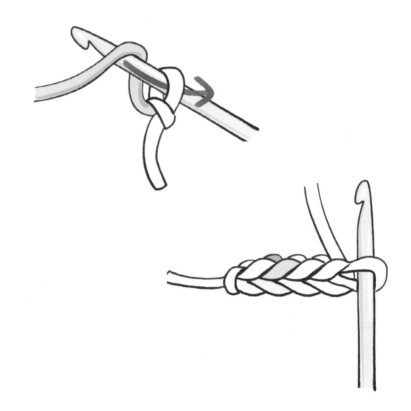

Front loop vs back loop

The tops of your crochet stitches form a row of V-shapes. The back loop is always furthest from you, while the front loop is closest. Unless a pattern tells you which loop to use, always crochet into both loops by inserting your hook underneath the entire V-shape.

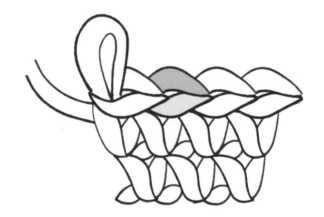

Inside vs outside

When working in the round, the front (outside) of a crochet piece will look different from the back (inside). The front of each stitch looks like a V-shape, while the back looks like an upside-down V with a horizontal bar on top.

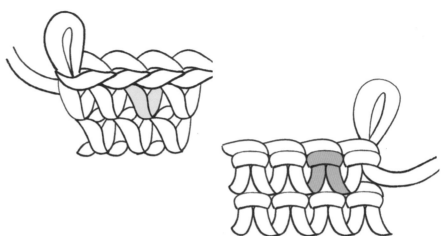

Counting stitches

Count the stitches by looking at the V-shape on top of each stitch. Each V counts as one stitch. The loop currently on your hook never counts as a stitch.

Slip stitch

Insert your hook into the desired stitch. Yarn over and draw the yarn through all loops on the hook.

Double crochet stitch

Insert your hook into the desired stitch. Yarn over and draw the yarn through the stitch (two loops left on hook). Yarn over and draw the yarn through both loops on the hook.

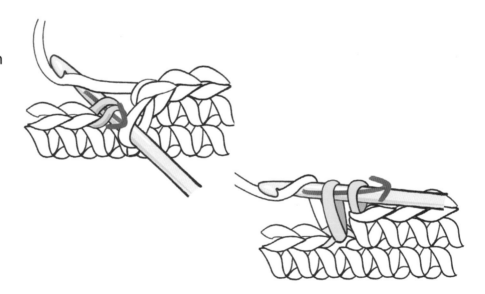

Half treble stitch

Yarn over and insert your hook into the desired stitch. Yarn over and draw the yarn through the stitch (three loops on hook). Yarn over and draw the yarn through all three loops on the hook.

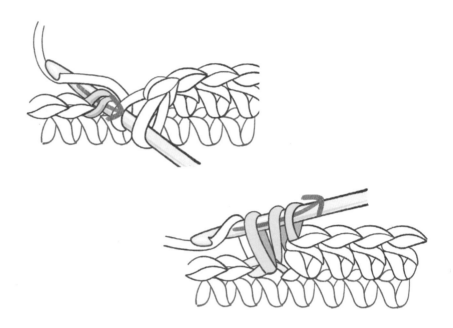

Treble stitch

Yarn over and insert your hook into the desired stitch. Yarn over and draw the yarn through the stitch (three loops on hook). Yarn over and draw yarn through the first two loops on the hook (two loops remaining). Yarn over and draw through both loops on the hook.

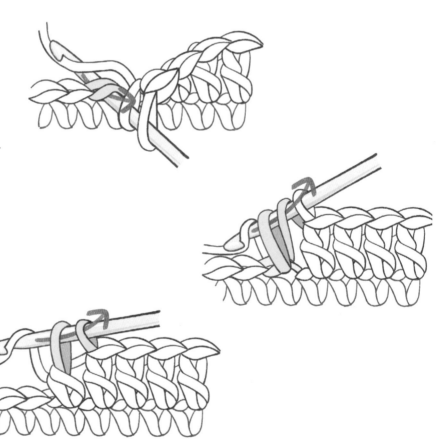

Double crochet two together

Insert your hook into the FRONT LOOP of the desired stitch, from bottom to top. Insert your hook into the FRONT LOOP of the next stitch (three loops on hook). Yarn over and draw yarn through two loops on your hook (two loops remaining). Yarn over and draw through both loops on hook. This technique is also called an invisible decrease.

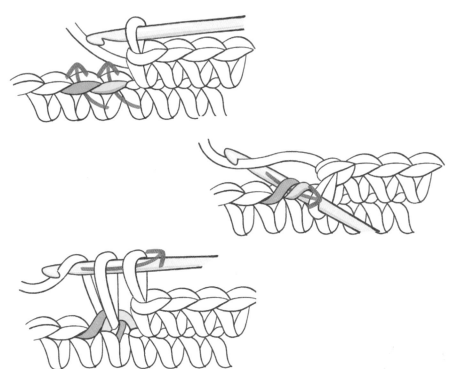

Finishing off

After completing the final stitch in the pattern, there will be one loop left on your hook. Cut the yarn, leaving an 8–12in (20–30cm) long tail for sewing. Pull up on the remaining loop until the yarn tail slips all the way through.

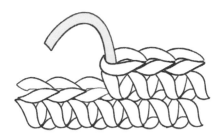

Close the hole

Work the final stitch, cut your yarn and finish off. Using a yarn needle, thread the yarn through the front loop of each remaining stitch, from bottom to top. Pull on the yarn to draw the hole closed. Thread the yarn into the middle of the hole, and out on the other end of the amigurumi's body. Tie a knot, cut away the excess yarn, and hide the knot inside the body.

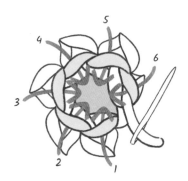

Join a round

Complete the final stitch, cut the yarn, and finish off. Thread the tail onto a needle. Skip the first stitch of the previous round, then thread your yarn through both loops of the next stitch, from front to back.

Thread your yarn through the back loop of the final stitch, from top to bottom. You have just created a V-shape stitch that looks just like all the other stitches. This is also called an invisible join.

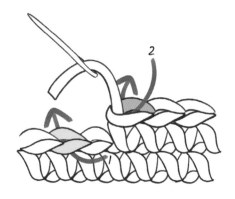

Join a new colour on a new round

Complete the final stitch in the old colour, and join the round with an invisible join. With the new colour, tie a slip knot around your crochet hook. Insert the hook into the stitch next to the join. Complete the first stitch of the new round as if your yarn were already joined. Hide the yarn tails on the inside of your amigurumi.

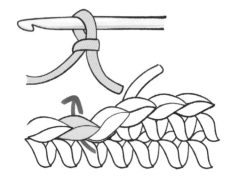

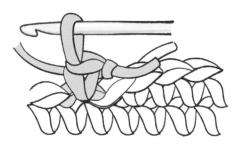

Sew crocheted pieces together

Use a blunt-tipped yarn needle to sew crocheted pieces onto the body. For small pieces with two yarn ends close together (like hands and small ears), simply sew both ends into the amigurumi body. Tie a knot in each end, and hide the knots inside the body.

For flat pieces (like feet and snouts), pin the piece in place against the amigurumi body. Pass your needle through a loop on the body, up through both loops of a stitch on the crocheted piece, then down through both loops of the next stitch. Repeat until you have worked your way around the entire piece.

For flat edges (like big ears and wings), hold the piece against the amigurumi body. Pass your needle underneath a stitch on the body, then up through a loop on the edge of the crocheted piece. Repeat until the entire edge is attached.

Embroidering facial features

Take a length of yarn or thread, tie a knot in one end, and thread the other end through your needle. Insert the needle anywhere on the amigurumi body and out where you want the first stitch to begin. Tug gently so that the knot end is hidden inside the amigurumi body. Embroider a stitch by inserting the needle into the body where you want the stitch to end, then out where you want the next stitch to begin. For eyes and noses, make a few stitches in the same place. To finish off, bring the needle out somewhere on the amigurumi's body, tie a knot, and hide the knot inside the body.

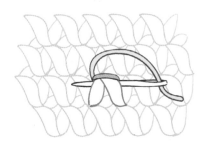

Cutting felt shapes

Trace the template from the book onto a piece of stiff card stock, and cut it out. Place the card template onto your felt, then use a fabric marker to trace around the edge. Cut the shape out using a pair of sharp scissors.

Sewing felt pieces in place

Pin the felt piece onto the amigurumi body. Take a length of thread, tie a knot in one end, and thread the other end through your needle. Insert the needle anywhere on the amigurumi body and out through the felt piece where you want the first stitch to begin. Tug gently so that the knot end is hidden inside the amigurumi body. Make a small stitch by inserting the needle into the amigurumi body next to the felt edge, then up through the felt where you want the next stitch to begin. Repeat until you have worked your way around the entire piece. Try to keep your stitches small and evenly spaced.

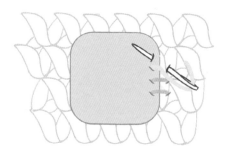

Abbreviations and conversions

Abbreviations

ch	chain
dc	double crochet
dc2tog	double crochet two stitches together
htr	half treble crochet
in	inches
m	metres
mm	millimetres
sl st	slip stitch
st(s)	stitch(es)
tog	together
tr	treble crochet
yd	yards

UK and US crochet terminology

The UK and the US use different names for many crochet stitches, which can be confusing if you are used to working in one system but are following a pattern written in the other 'language'.

This book is written using UK terms; below we list the US equivalents. These stitches are listed in height order, from shortest to tallest.

UK	US
Double crochet	Single crochet
Half treble	Half double crochet
Treble	Double crochet
Double treble	Triple crochet
Treble treble	Double triple crochet

Crochet hook sizes

All the patterns in this book are written using a size 3.5mm (UK9/USE/4) crochet hook. However, if you would like to experiment with varying the size of your crochet creature, here is a complete table of crochet hook sizes in all three systems.

UK	Metric	US
14	2mm	–
13	2.25mm	B/1
12	2.5mm	–
–	2.75mm	C/2
11	3mm	–
10	3.25mm	D/3
9	3.5mm	E/4
–	3.75mm	F/5
8	4mm	G/6
7	4.5mm	7
6	5mm	H/8
5	5.5mm	I/9
4	6mm	J/10
3	6.5mm	K/10.5
2	7mm	–
0	8mm	L/11
00	9mm	M–N/13
000	10mm	N–P/15

Yarn weights

All the projects in this book are made in medium-weight yarn using a size 3.5mm (UK9/USE/4) crochet hook. This is a smaller size hook than is usually recommended for that weight of yarn: this is a deliberate choice to create a dense fabric that won't show the stuffing inside the creature.

Feel free to experiment with different weights of yarn to create larger or smaller animals. Here is a guide to yarn weight conversions:

UK	US
1 ply	Laceweight
2 ply	Fingering
3 ply	Sock
4 ply	Sport
DK	DK/Light Worsted
Aran	Worsted
Chunky	Bulky
Super Chunky	Super Bulky

Suppliers and resources

You can buy yarn and crochet hooks from numerous retail outlets and online suppliers. Many will ship worldwide. Here are just a few.

UK

Black Sheep Wools Ltd
Warehouse Studios
Glaziers Lane
Culcheth
Warrington
WA3 4AQ
+44 (0)1925 764231
www.blacksheepwools.com

Fred Aldous Ltd
37 Lever St
Manchester
M1 1Lw
+44 (0)161 236 4224
or
34 Kirkgate
Leeds
LS2 7DR
+44 (0)113 243 3531
www.fredaldous.co.uk

Hobbycraft
Stores nationwide
+44 0330 026 1400
www.hobbycraft.co.uk

Laughing Hens
The Croft Stables
Station Lane
Great Barrow
Cheshire
CH3 7JN
+44 (0)1829 740903
www.laughinghens.com

Love Crochet
www.lovecrochet.com
+44 (0)845 544 2196

Rowan
MEZ Crafts UK
17F Brooke's Mill,
Armitage Bridge
Huddersfield
West Yorkshire
HD4 7NR
+44 (0)1484 950630
www.knitrowan.com

Stylecraft
Spectrum Yarns
Spa Mill
Slaithwaite
Huddersfield
West Yorkshire
HD7 5BB
+44 (0)1484 848435
www.stylecraft-yarns.co.uk

USA

Michaels
1-800-642-4235
www.michaels.com

Purl soho
459 Broome Street
New York 10013
+1 212 420 8796
www.purlsoho.com

The Knitting Garden
1923 Ponce De Leon Blvd
Coral Gables FL 33134
+1 305 774 1060
www.theknittinggarden.org

Inspirational Websites
Search 'amigurumi' on the Internet and you will find a vast array of sources of inspiration. Pinterest and Instragram are great for getting ideas, while Attic 24 is the ideal blog to peruse if you're new to crochet.

Attic24
www.attic24.typepad.com

Instragram
www.instagram.com

Pinterest
www.pinterest.com

About the author

Lauren Bergstrom is a South African amigurumi artist, currently living on an island in Canada. She learnt to crochet over 20 years ago but her love of the craft was reignited through her discovery of amigurumi.

In 2011 Lauren created mohumohu.com, which is an online store and blog offering amigurumi toys, patterns and crochet tutorials. At first, it was just a creative outlet for Lauren while she completed her music degree at university, but she found she couldn't stop making woolly creatures, and eventually her hobby became a full-time career.

Lauren's work is inspired by real-life animals, kawaii culture, and anything small and cute. When she's not making amigurumi, she enjoys knitting, sewing, needle felting, painting and drawing.

Index

A
abbreviations 154
adjustable ring 145

B
back loop 146
Bear 100–103
Bunny 34–37
Butterfly 78–81

C
Cat 38–41
Caterpillar 82–85
Chick 12–15
Chicken 16–19
close the amigurumi hole 149
conversions 154
counting stitches 147
Cow 20–23
crochet
    stitches 147–149
    terminology 154
cutting felt shapes 152

D
Dog 42–45
double crochet
    stitch 147
    two together 149

E
Elephant 122–125
embroider facial features 151

F
facial features, embroider 151
Farm animals 10–31
felt shapes, cutting 152
finishing off 149
foundation chain 146
Fox 104–107
front loop 146

G
Goldfish 46–49
Guinea pig 50–53

H
half treble stitch 148
Hippo 126–129
hole, closing the amigurumi 149
Honey bee 86–89
hook
    holding 144
    sizes 155

I
inside 'v' shape 147
invisible join 150

J
join
    invisible 150
    new colour 150
    round 150

L
Ladybird 90–93
Lion 130–133
Little animals 76–97

M
materials 142–143

O
Otter 60–63
outside 'v' shape 147
Owl 108–111

P
Panda 134–137
Penguin 56–59
Pet animals 32–53
Piglet 24–27

R
Raccoon 112–115
ring, adjustable 145
round
    join 150
    new colour 150

S

Sea
   animals 54–75
   bunny 64–67
Seal 68–71
sew
   felt in place 152
   pieces together 151
sewing techniques 151–152
Sheep 28–31
slip knot 145
slip stitch 147
Sloth 138–141
Snail 94–97
Squirrel 116–119
stitch counting 147

T

techniques 144–152
templates
   chicken face 18
   elephant ear 124
   fox face 106
   guinea pig eye patch 52
   lion snout 132
   otter snout 62
   owl face 110
   panda eye patch 136
   penguin eye 58
   raccoon face and mask
      114
   sheep face 30
   sloth eye and face 140
   squirrel tummy 118
   using 152
terminology, crochet 154
tools 142–143
treble stitch 148

W

Whale 72–75
Woodland animals 98–119

Y

yarn
   holding 144
   over 145
   weights 155

Z

Zoo animals 120–141

To order a book, or to request
a catalogue, contact:

GMC Publications Ltd
Castle Place
166 High Street
Lewes, East Sussex
BN7 1XU
United Kingdom
Tel: +44 (0)1273 488005
www.gmcbooks.com